W9-ACA-547

The Government Factor

The Government Factor

Undermining Journalistic Ethics in the Information Age

Richard T. Kaplar and Patrick D. Maines

CATO INSTITUTE

Washington, D.C.

Library of Congress Cataloging-in-Publication Data

Kaplar, Richard T.
    The government factor : undermining journalistic ethics in the
information age / Richard T. Kaplar and Patrick D. Maines.
        p.   cm.
    Includes bibliographical references.
    ISBN 1-882577-25-6. — ISBN 1-882577-26-4 (pbk.)
    1. Journalistic ethics—United States.   2. Freedom of the press—
United States.   3. Government and the press—United States.   4. Mass
media—United States—Moral and ethical aspects.   I. Maines, Patrick
D.   II. Title.
PN4888.E8K37   1995
174'.9097—dc20   95-19720
                                                                              CIP

Cover Design by Randy White.

Printed in the United States of America.

CATO INSTITUTE
1000 Massachusetts Ave., N.W.
Washington, D.C. 20001

Contents

Foreword

This monograph is the first in a series of studies to be published as part of the Cato Institute's **Project on Civil Society.** The purpose of the project is to increase public understanding and practice of the rules of just conduct that form the basis for a free and prosperous society.

The rules that guide society and the concept of justice inherent in those rules are important determinants of the social, political, and economic order. In the liberal tradition, a just society is one that safeguards individual rights to life, liberty, and property. A good society, however, goes beyond protecting our right to be left alone; there is more to morality and civility than simply respecting negative rights. Right conduct and good manners are as important as good laws.

In a free society, benevolence—though not required by law— makes everyday life more humane and society more civil. We have a right to pursue our values as long as we do not violate the equal rights of others. However, if freedom is not accompanied by virtue, freedom will turn into license and endanger civil society.

Civil society is the result of the voluntary joining together of different individuals to further common goals. The churches, clubs, charities, and associations (both educational and business) that people join constitute a social network that is independent of government and that cultivates community life.

What holds civil society together is not the weak bond of legislation but the strong bonds of friendship and mutual interests. Social and economic harmony require a rule of law, open markets, and voluntary adherence to morals and manners. The formal legal structure of society will not be sufficient to create a just society, a prosperous economy, and a vibrant community unless it is fortified by basic ethical principles, a sense of responsibility, and respect for persons and property.

The growth of government has eroded traditional values by making individuals more dependent and less self-reliant. The welfare state has undermined individual responsibility, and the regulatory state has hampered free-market solutions to social and economic problems.

Richard Kaplar and Patrick Maines discuss how government regulation has impeded the development of journalistic ethics and how increased competition and new technology promise to improve standards of conduct in both the electronic and print media. Such improvement, they contend, will require that government get out of the way of the market and not try to block the substitution of private for government ethics in journalism.

The Cato Institute gratefully acknowledges the generous support of the Claude R. Lambe Charitable Foundation, which was responsible for initiating the Project on Civil Society.

—JAMES A. DORN
Director, Project on Civil Society

Preface

The development of journalistic ethics is an enterprise crisscrossed by an intricate web of tensions between and among competing forces, both inside and outside of journalism. Some of these forces (like competing philosophies) are immediately obvious; others (such as economics, technology, and regulation) come into focus upon reflection.

Consider some of the myriad tensions: Practical, tough-minded journalists are often at odds with philosopher academicians and their abstract theories. Among journalists, meanwhile, the tension between print reporters and their broadcast counterparts is palpable. In the newsroom, ethical principles compete with the need for attention-grabbing coverage in the shaping of editorial decisions. Journalists' constitutional guarantees of free speech and a free press conflict with their subjects' rights to privacy and freedom from defamation. In the bigger picture, society wrestles with the concept of a free press versus a responsible press. And the technological revolution that has given us the information age creates constant tension between the status quo and inevitable change, down to our very concept of who journalists are and what they do.

In a society as complex as ours, a discussion of journalistic ethics cannot occur solely in the isolated realm of the theoretical (though it must begin there), nor even, as it usually does, in the context of applying ethical principles to newsroom situations. Rather, ethical discussion must take place in the broader context of society itself, mindful of the social, economic, governmental, and technological forces that define the newsroom well before the newsroom is able to define its ethical stance.

The purpose of this monograph is to examine one of those forces—government intervention (in the form of laws and communications policy)—and its effect on the media's ethical decisionmaking. Our premise is that government interferes in the formation of journalistic ethics in two ways: first (and overtly) by imposing laws and regulations that have the effect of substituting government ethics for private ethics; and second (and more subtly) by erecting structural barriers that hinder the development of media that would be more hospitable to ethical conduct. Government has no more business regulating the competitive development of the communications industry than it does regulating program content. Yet it continues to do both with great abandon.

The role of government in regulating the communications industry is well documented, but the impact of this regulation on the development of journalistic ethics has been largely overlooked. We hope this monograph begins to draw attention to this pernicious situation—and does so before regulators succeed in dictating the structure and content of the "information superhighway" that looms ahead.

Acknowledgments

We wish to acknowledge the tireless research assistance of Andrew Auerbach, staff attorney of the Media Institute, whose thoroughness and attention to detail were highly valued.

We also wish to thank communications attorneys J. Laurent Scharff, Sol Schildhause, and Richard M. Schmidt Jr., and journalism ethicist Jay Black, for reviewing early drafts of the manuscript. We would not expect any of them to embrace everything we say herein, but their willingness to share their considerable expertise has added greatly to this publication. Sol Schildhause was especially helpful in recounting an oral history of developments at the Federal Communications Commission during his tenure as its first "cable czar" in the 1960s and 1970s.

Finally, we would like to thank the Cato Institute for giving us the opportunity to put these thoughts in print. Cato's belief that the communications industry is best left alone by government is remarkably similar to our own. The leadership of Ed Crane and the fine editorial hand of Jim Dorn allowed us to bring this book from concept to fruition.

1. Introduction

From cocktail parties to classrooms, "journalistic ethics" has become a hot topic of conversation in recent times. *NBC Nightly News* illustrated a story on water pollution in an Idaho forest with pictures of fish from another location that looked dead but had actually been stunned.[1] A reporter and cameraman at a local station in Minnesota were fired after they bought teenagers two cases of beer for a story on underage drinking.[2] *Dateline NBC* rigged a pickup truck with incendiary devices to make sure it exploded on cue in a test crash.[3]

And the "tabloid journalism" purveyed by syndicated shows like *A Current Affair* has begun seeping into network prime time—and even into the networks' nightly newscasts. During the 1994 Winter Olympics, for instance, CBS's flagship evening news program placed the Tonya Harding affair on center stage, with Connie Chung conducting exclusive interviews with the figure skater in Lillehammer as if that were a hard news story instead of a tawdry sidebar to a sports story. Even *Newsweek* looked at the television landscape and asked in a cover headline: "TV's news war: Stooping too low?"[4]

The networks answered with a resounding "yes" once again as the O.J. Simpson story unfolded. TV news professionals scrambled to broadcast the most outlandish snippets of speculation, opinion, and information (confirmed or not), and preempted prime-time programming for live coverage of Simpson's Los Angeles freeway escapade.

On another front, journalistic ethics have been debated seriously and with growing interest among academicians, journalists, and

[1]Howard Kurtz and John Carmody, "NBC Exec Ousted Over Staged Crash," *Washington Post*, March 3, 1993, p. A1.

[2]Howard Kurtz, "Education Reporter Gets School Job, Lesson in Ethics," *Washington Post*, February 25, 1993, p. D1.

[3]Elizabeth Kolbert, "NBC Admits Bad Judgment in Truck Report," *New York Times*, March 23, 1993, p. D23.

[4]*Newsweek*, April 11, 1994.

1

journalism organizations. In 1993 the Society of Professional Journalists (SPJ) published a handbook, after years of effort, titled *Doing Ethics in Journalism.*[5] The Associated Press Managing Editors struggled mightily to develop a new code of ethics featuring detailed guidelines on appropriate conduct (but finally agreed to an updated statement of general principles). And, as John C. Merrill and S. Jack Odell observe, "At long last, philosophical dimensions of journalism are beginning to compete in public discourse and academic circles with psychological and sociological perspectives which have dominated such discourse since the 1930s."[6]

Such attention is long overdue, but alas, much of the effort appears shrouded in vagueness and ambiguity. Many books on journalistic ethics are little more than collections of case studies that serve to illustrate prevailing conventions but do little to relate journalistic practices to underlying ethical principles. The fact that journalists agree to consider a certain practice "ethical" means only that they have agreed to agree and nothing more; lacking a framework built on classical ethical theory and moral reasoning, there is no way to judge a practice on a meaningful ethical level.

We try to address that problem here by beginning with an outline of classical ethical theory—the sort of foundation missing from too many books on the subject. "Ethics" means many things to many people, and we did not wish to write a monograph on journalistic ethics that danced around the topic without saying what, at bottom, ethical principles are and how they come to be formed. It is not our purpose, however, to try to arrive at a comprehensive system of journalistic ethics, or to presume to tell journalists what their ethical standards ought to be. (The scope of our concern is, in fact, limited for the most part to those aspects of journalistic ethics dealing with accuracy, fairness, and privacy, but even here we are not setting ourselves up as arbiters of ethical conduct—that is something journalists must do for themselves.)

Rather, we wish to focus on one aspect of journalistic ethics that has, we feel, been largely overlooked in texts on the subject: the role

---

[5] Jay Black, Bob Steele, and Ralph Barney, *Doing Ethics in Journalism: A Handbook With Case Studies* (Greencastle, Ind.: Sigma Delta Chi Foundation and Society of Professional Journalists, 1993).

[6] John C. Merrill and S. Jack Odell, *Philosophy and Journalism* (New York: Longman, 1983), p. ix.

of government in the process of ethical decisionmaking. Government plays a role in two ways; the first is through laws and regulations that affect the program content of broadcast media, and that affect the editorial process for all journalists in the areas of defamation and invasion of privacy. We call this phenomenon "the substitution of 'government ethics' for private ethics" because these government mandates tend to supersede journalists' own standards as the basis for editorial decisionmaking.

The second way government interferes in the ethics process is by creating structural barriers to the development of the technologies that may be more hospitable to ethical conduct. Cable television, for example, seems to offer an environment with more opportunities for the practice of ethical journalism compared with the broadcast networks, for a variety of reasons that we discuss in Chapter 4. Yet for years Congress and the Federal Communications Commission stifled the development of cable. Even today the FCC is in the process of enforcing rate regulations that are slowing the provision of scores of new program services and hindering cable's ability to start building the "information superhighway" of the next century.

We would not make the claim that most ethical lapses by journalists are caused by government interference. Nor would we claim the opposite—that, lacking government impediments, journalism would be an ethical paradise. But we do think that the influence of government on journalistic ethics is onerous and counterproductive, especially at a time when the development of new technologies promises to redefine our concept of journalistic ethics and place new demands on journalists and ethicists alike.

Journalistic ethics have traditionally been discussed in the context of the individual—the process of moral reasoning through which a journalist arrives at a decision in a given situation. As technologies of communication become more fragmented and structurally diverse, however, we suggest it may be time to devote more attention to the influence of those technologies on the practice of journalism and on journalistic ethics. The nexus of technological medium and journalistic practice will of necessity command the attention of ethicists in the years ahead.

Just as the ethical perspective must broaden in response to new technologies, we would also ask journalism professors and ethicists to consider the overlooked role of government in the ethical decisionmaking process, and to expand ethical debate to include this reality.

To do so may open up some exciting new vistas of ethical discussion. For example, what will be the ethical impact on print journalists when their product is delivered via an electronic medium that is subject to broadcast-style regulation? To what degree can government regulators of the information superhighway be expected to assess the effect of their actions on journalistic ethics? From where will government derive the moral authority to impose laws and regulations that take the place of ethically reasoned standards, or that stifle the climate in which moral reasoning can take place?

We cannot hope to answer such questions in this publication. We do, however, attempt to give the reader a better understanding of the relationship between ethical decisionmaking and the counterproductive role of government. Chapter 2 traces the outlines of classical ethical theory, explores the difficulties that journalists face in dealing with ethicists and ethical theory, and discusses some hopeful attempts at integrating ethical theory with practical decisionmaking. Chapter 3 looks at ways in which this vibrant process of ethical development suffers when "government ethics" in the form of broadcast content controls, libel law, and other government regulations are substituted for private ethics. Chapter 4 examines yet another way government interferes in the ethics process—by erecting structural barriers that stifle the growth of the very media that may offer greater opportunities for ethical conduct. And Chapter 5 warns of the deleterious effects of such government meddling on the nascent information superhighway.

In summary, it appears that the debate on journalistic ethics between journalists and academicians is becoming even more robust. This is a hopeful sign, but the process is being hindered significantly by the intervention of government in ways that are often overlooked and underdiscussed. Some might argue that none of this matters all that much. In his recently published memoirs, John Corry, a 30-year veteran (and former media critic) of the *New York Times*, takes a dim view of efforts like those we describe in Chapter 2: "The sole function of journalism is to inform and entertain, and while this is honorable, it is not elevated, and abstruse moral discussions about the trade are for the birds."[7] But perhaps all journalists could find common

---

[7]John Corry, *My Times: Adventures in the News Trade* (New York: G.P. Putnam's Sons, 1993), p. 16.

ground by approaching this monograph from a slightly different perspective. We would ask them to be mindful of an indisputable fact usually stated in a First Amendment context that applies with equal force to ethics: Government involvement in the editorial process is undesirable and even dangerous, and must be resisted at all cost.

2. The Dynamic Process of Ethics

The allegations were serious. General Motors pickup trucks made between 1973 and 1987 were killing passengers needlessly because the vehicles tended to burst into flames and explode when involved in side-impact collisions. The culprits were side-mounted fuel tanks, hung on the outside of the frame rails and thus easily punctured in a crash. Yet GM seemed oblivious to this incredible design flaw, more interested in putting thousands of unwitting buyers behind the wheels of these popularly styled deathtraps than in the safety of the driving public.

These are the allegations that viewers of *Dateline NBC* would infer on November 17, 1992. The title of the segment, "Waiting to Explode," left little doubt that the show's producers had no lingering questions about GM's guilt. The facts, after all, spoke for themselves. What viewers *saw* on that segment made it an airtight case against GM.

Dateline NBC had hired an outside firm to conduct a test crash in which an automobile would slam into the side of a GM pickup. Car met truck, there was a puff of smoke and then, sure enough, a fire broke out and quickly engulfed the side of the truck. Could there be any doubt that these pickups were anything but the "rolling firebombs" that *Dateline NBC* claimed? The program had made its case and rendered the verdict. GM was guilty. The pictures didn't lie.

Or did they? What *Dateline NBC* failed to tell its viewers was that the crash had been rigged. In fact, the outside contractor had staged two explosion attempts. The first produced the fire shown on the air, not because the fuel tank had ruptured, but because an ill-fitting replacement filler cap had allowed fuel to spray from the filler pipe. The second attempt produced nothing—no rupture, no explosion, nothing consistent with NBC's allegations. The *Washington Post* reported that *Dateline NBC* correspondent Michelle Gillen had reservations about using the footage but was overruled by her producer, Jeff Diamond. But when the segment aired, as *Post* writer Benjamin Weiser noted:

7

Gillen did not say the fire lasted 15 seconds. She did not say
the fire went out on its own. She did not say that "Dateline"
had reversed the order of the crashes so that the demonstra-
tion culminated in a burst of fire, rather than a dud. She did
not say that the gasoline tank's cap was a replacement that
may not have properly fit, which could have been the reason
it flew off and allowed gasoline to escape.[1]

And Gillen did not say that the contractor had rigged the test truck
with model rocket engines, small incendiary devices resembling
miniature road flares. An investigation by outside attorneys commissioned by NBC in the aftermath concluded that "the desire to tape
a crash fire was as important to the decision to do the test as was
the desire to determine whether the trucks were unsafe. In pursuing
this goal 'Dateline' journalists did not believe they were consciously
doing something wrong, but the goal was enough to cause them to
fall short of the careful evaluation of their plans."[2]

How could TV journalists broadcast a deceptive crash test involving a rigged vehicle, fail to mention key facts about test conditions,
imply that the bogus test bolstered their allegations about the unwor-
thiness of GM pickup trucks, and "not believe they were doing
something consciously wrong"? What ethical considerations ani-
mated their decisions? Most likely they were not motivated by ethical
concerns at all, but by the dictates and conventions of TV "news
magazine" shows that have as much, or more, to do with entertainment as with news. As journalism ethicist Jeffrey Olen puts it:

> An eye for drama may easily be confused with news judg-
> ment. And a search for pictures may be confused with a
> search for the heart of a story. When television news divisions
> insist, as a matter of policy, that drama be part of every story,
> these dangers grow greater.[3]

Is it any wonder that the credibility of journalists continues to
decline? The furor that erupted over this *Dateline NBC* episode clearly

---

[1]Benjamin Weiser, "Does TV News Go Too Far?" *Washington Post*, February 28,
1993, p. A1.

[2]Elizabeth Kolbert, "NBC Admits Bad Judgment in Truck Report," *New York Times*,
March 23, 1993, p. D23.

[3]Jeffrey Olen, *Ethics in Journalism* (Englewood Cliffs, N.J.: Prentice-Hall, 1988),
pp. 110–11.

demonstrates the need for an ethical framework, at the very least a framework that respects intuitive sensibilities about truth and fairness. This segment has become a rallying point for those who would say that ethics among journalists is like virtue among prostitutes. And at bottom this episode illustrates the sizable gap that exists between philosophers and journalists, between principled ethical considerations and the practical dilemmas of producing stories that people will watch and read.

Of Philosophers and Journalists

Before we can contemplate where journalistic ethics may be headed in a new media age, it would be helpful to consider the state of ethics in the current age. How has ethics evolved as a force in journalistic decisionmaking? How important are ethical considerations in the lives of working journalists? How important a role should ethics play, and what ethical framework should be employed?

If there seems to be a tension between ethics and journalism, if the application of ethics to journalism seems uncertain or inadequate or even irrelevant, it is because ethics and journalism are, in some key respects, strange bedfellows. Ethics is the branch of philosophy concerned with moral decisionmaking. What puts it at odds with journalism is not that ethics deals with moral questions, but that it is a branch of philosophy.

Philosophy is a discipline that operates in the realm of the theoretical; journalism operates in the precinct houses and courthouses of the real world. Good philosophers have a capacity for abstract thinking; among journalists the ability to think and express thoughts in concrete terms is prized. Philosophical discussions tend to be open ended in scope and ongoing in duration; the great questions about the nature of being and meaning of existence remain open to discussion thousands of years after Aristotle and Socrates. Journalism, in contrast, seeks to present information with a sense of finality while meeting deadlines that are clearly finite in nature. "And that's the way it is," as Walter Cronkite would assure us each night. Philosophy is a contemplative activity while journalism is action oriented.

Perhaps as a result of these differences, each camp has looked askance at the other, with each striking a pose of superiority. As Jay Newman has observed:

Most of the great philosophers periodically touched upon subjects as concrete, as practical, and as prosaic as the subject of journalism. And yet, journalism as such rarely received direct attention from those among them who were familiar with it, and the tradition of neglecting journalism has been carried on by most of their contemporary successors.[4]

At the risk of overgeneralizing, it would not be stretching too far to say that philosophers have preferred to think of themselves as thoughtful and erudite compared with journalists, whom they perceive to be unfocused if not downright ignorant and in any event barely removed from the unwashed masses. Journalists, on the other hand, think of themselves as quick-witted pragmatists; they take pride in turning out a useful product under difficult conditions, and think of philosophers as idle dreamers whose practical contributions to society are highly questionable. One philosopher related his perception of the working scribe thus:

Perhaps the journalist, as much as anyone in our society, is in a position to lose his selfhood and conform. . . . He may feel himself creative, but the nature of his work routinizes him into patterns of activity devoid of creativity, challenge, spontaneity, and potency. His perception of the world is from the circumscribed view of the journalistic institution. He does his job, mechanically (or mechanistically) day after day without showing many—if any—sparks of creativity and passion. In fact, lack of passion—a *dispassionate* demeanor—is what defines his natural journalistic state.[5]

Yet reporters and editors gazing from the newsroom to academe are hardly wistful. As one journalist summed it up:

I don't think it's sensible to define journalism in intellectual terms that more correctly belong within the field of the novelist as they relate to a philosophical train of thought—i.e., Dostoyevsky, Camus, Sartre, Ibsen, Melville. Journalism has, or ought to have, an immediate impact on social problems. One doesn't tell a welfare mother or an unemployed worker that they are "Part of History. . . ." For the present

[4]Jay Newman, *The Journalist in Plato's Cave* (Cranbury, N.J.: Associated University Presses, 1989), p. 15.

[5]John C. Merrill, *Existential Journalism* (New York: Hastings House, 1977), pp. 20–21 (emphasis in original).

I am too busy doing whatever I do, to bother with what I think I think I'm doing.[6]

Despite these differences in outlook and temperament, philosophers and journalists have in recent years shown signs of working together, especially in the field of ethics. Indicative of this trend was the launching of a new publication, *Journal of Mass Media Ethics*, which arrived on the scene in late 1985. A number of books linking the practice of journalism to philosophical and ethical concerns have also appeared in recent years. One of them, *Philosophy and Journalism*, makes a modest though eminently realistic claim regarding the benefit of applying philosophy to the journalistic craft: "Philosophy—or a concern for philosophizing—will not automatically eliminate cynicism or a pessimistic *Weltanschauung*, but it will push the journalist's thinking into more systematic and logical channels and provide a more coherent foundation for his journalistic belief and value system."[7]

Journalism, it has been said, is most influenced by the branches of philosophy known as logic, semantics, epistemology, and ethics. Logic provides the fundamental methodology of philosophy, allowing us to recognize reasoning that is true and dismiss reasoning that is false. Semantics, also known as conceptual analysis, is another methodological tool that allows us to clarify thought by clarifying the meaning of words. Epistemology addresses the nature of what we know. Many of the great philosophical questions (e.g., about existence, truth, and reality) are in fact epistemological questions. These three fields would appear to have some direct benefit to journalism if their study leads journalists to think and reason logically, express thoughts precisely, and have a deeper understanding of what we know and how we come to know it. None of these three branches is more important to the practice of journalism, however, than ethics, and that shall be the focus of our discussion herein. As Merrill and Odell note, "Stupid journalists simply misinform us; unethical ones also deceive us."[8]

---

[6]Quoted in Merrill, p. 26.

[7]John C. Merrill and S. Jack Odell, *Philosophy and Journalism* (New York: Longman, 1983), p. x.

[8]Ibid., p. 2.

Schools of Ethical Thought

Ethics in journalism has been a subject of heightened interest recently among journalists and journalism organizations and has proved especially durable as a conference topic among both professors and working journalists. There is a great deal of interest in "improving" journalistic ethics, although a paradoxical situation has become evident. Journalists as a group are quite independent, mindful of the constitutional protection afforded their craft, and thus reluctant to let anyone tell them what to do. Newman said that journalists "often reveal an ignorance of their subject matter that is rooted in their refusal to learn from the most thoughtful and disciplined writers on moral and political subjects."[9]

Suggestions for "ethical improvements" that emanate from outside the craft are immediately suspect and are generally assumed to be thinly veiled attempts to impose on journalists one set or another of ideological beliefs. For example, outsiders' suggestions extolling the virtues of objectivity and balance, especially in the context of correcting a "liberal media bias," are assumed to be conservative in origin. Calling for a "responsible press," on the other hand, can be viewed as conservative or liberal, and particularly the latter if the suggested remedy involves oversight or some other action by government.

Ethical improvements suggested by professors may not be as suspect on ideological grounds but are rather easily dismissed as being good in theory but not very applicable to the situations and problems a journalist confronts in a day's work. That applies only slightly less to professors of journalism and mass communication than it does to professors of philosophy. Journalists seem to give the most credence, then, to the views of other journalists and perhaps especially to the "elder statesmen" among them.

Certainly a long career in journalism will yield many practical insights and probably even a homespun philosophy about how the craft should be practiced. What is missing in much of the literature and most of the dialogue, however, is a sense of the craft's philosophical underpinnings—a recognition of how journalistic conventions and written guidelines (the practical expressions of ethical standards) are related to the larger ethical principles and values that transcend journalism.

[9]Newman, p. 19.

Journalists seem oddly content to deal with ethical questions on a case-by-case basis. Indeed, many books on journalistic ethics are primarily collections of case studies that give the reader a chance to judge how someone else handled a situation with ethical over-tones—a sort of "you make the call" for reporters. Would you take that free lunch? Would you let your source read a draft of your story? Is it okay to let people assume you're someone other than a reporter as long as you don't lie outright about your identity? Can you go ahead and lie if you have to?

Case studies contribute to journalism's body of knowledge about itself and are the precedents that help form journalistic conventions (i.e., informal standards or "oral traditions"), many of which find their way into written guidelines and codes of conduct. Most case-study approaches prove unsatisfactory from a philosophical stand-point, however, because of their obvious limitations. Case studies can be either descriptive (telling us how someone dealt with an ethical issue) or normative (telling us how the person *should* have dealt with it). But their frame of reference is generally limited to journalistic conventions, those informal standards based on practical experience that evolve over time out of journalism's collective con-science. Conventions can fall short, however, because they are not necessarily rooted in a valid ethical tradition or even based on true reasoning. The most we can say about conventions developed in an ad hoc manner is that most journalists agree that they should be followed, that is, that they are true. The fact that journalists agree they are true doesn't actually mean they *are* true (i.e., rooted in a valid ethical tradition)—it means only that agreement exists, correct or incorrect.

A convention may state, for example, that a journalist should never accept a free lunch. That convention may be based on a principle such as "Journalists should be independent and should not allow themselves to be compromised." But this still falls short because we must probe further: "What is the basis for this principle of indepen-dence? What ethical rationale are we relying on to favor indepen-dence over nonindependence?" At this point many journalists would be stumped and much of the literature on journalistic ethics wouldn't be of much help.

Yet if we are to fathom where journalistic ethics may be heading, and if we are to recognize the external (i.e., government) forces currently buffeting the ethical ship, we must have some understanding of how journalistic principles are related to the major schools of thought that constitute the ethics branch of philosophy—and that transcend applications to journalism. Classical ethical theory is divided into two broad camps—teleological and deontological. We shall begin by discussing some of the major ethical theories that are teleological in nature.

Teleological Theories of Ethics

A system of ethics that judges an action on the basis of the action's consequences is considered teleological. If a dictatorship decides to impound emergency food supplies that relief agencies have shipped in to nourish famine victims, thereby causing continued starvation and death, and if we judge the dictatorship's action to be wrong, we have judged the rightness or wrongness of that action on teleological grounds.

Teleological theories can be further divided as either egoistic or altruistic. Egoistic theories judge the rightness or wrongness of an action on whether the consequences of the action are beneficial to oneself. Thus, according to an egoistic approach the correct (or "right") ethical decision is the one that generates the greatest benefit for the decisionmaker. The reporter who seeks to advance his career by "scooping" rival reporters covering the same beat would be an example. A reporter could justify a whole range of actions on egoistic grounds—monopolizing the only phone line from a remote story site, for example, or even cutting the line when finished to prevent other reporters from filing their stories—if he thought such actions would result in the greatest benefit to himself.

Other teleological theories are altruistic. The most well known of these is called utilitarianism and was developed by Jeremy Bentham, an 18th-century philosopher. The guiding principle of utilitarianism is "Act so as to produce the greatest possible balance of good over evil in the world." If we define "good over evil" as "pleasure over pain" we are referring to hedonistic utilitarianism. Bentham himself described utilitarianism as striving for the "greatest happiness for the greatest number." Another concept of hedonistic utilitarianism was advanced by John Stuart Mill, who favored an emphasis on the quality of happiness over quantity. Throwing Christians to the lions would be justified by the hedonistic utilitarian as a right decision

14

because the carnage would bring pleasure to the spectators—provided there were more spectators than Christians to ensure a preponderance of pleasure over pain.

Another form of utilitarianism is nonhedonistic. Proponents of this school would contend that an action should be measured by criteria other than obtaining the greatest pleasure. Socrates, for example, argued that self-knowledge is the ultimate goal. Others might argue that the highest good is social harmony, or scientific knowledge, or return on investment. Many forms of nonhedonistic utilitarianism are possible.

Having sliced utilitarianism one way, as hedonistic or nonhedonistic, we can now slice it another—as either "act utilitarianism" or "rule utilitarianism." Act utilitarianism holds that an action should be judged on the basis of its consequences. The right act is the one whose consequences will live up to the utilitarian ideal by bringing about the greatest good. Thus, the act utilitarian will compare one possible action to another, weighing the probable consequences of each, and selecting the one having the most favorable outcome.

The rule utilitarian, on the other hand, is concerned not with the consequences of an action but with following the rule or precept that is likely to produce the greatest good. The rule utilitarian does not have to bother weighing one action against another; rather, he will determine the rule that has, by being followed in the past, produced the greatest good in that situation. It is then only a matter of acting in accordance with that rule. The act utilitarian, in contrast, sees acting according to rules as too uncertain a means of guaranteeing the best possible outcome. The key distinction is that act utilitarianism is future oriented whereas rule utilitarianism is past oriented. Act utilitarianism consists of predicting a consequence that is likely to occur at some point in the future if a certain action is taken now; rule utilitarianism, on the other hand, involves acting in accordance with a rule that has proved, from past experience, to yield the most desirable outcome.

Shortcomings in Teleological Theories

All the forms of teleological theories we have examined can be shown to have shortcomings of some degree as they are applied to everyday life—and to life in the newsroom. The weakness inherent in egoism should be fairly self-evident: It is the theory that everyone

15

should act in his or her own self-interest. One could imagine the result in a complex society such as ours, dependent as it is on interrelationships and transactions of all types among its members, if everyone pursued a strict self-interest. At one end of the spectrum some of the most important and selfless actions in society would go undone. Who would want to bother raising and educating children, caring for the elderly and underprivileged, or working on public service projects for the betterment of the community?

At the other end of the spectrum anarchy would result if people believed it were in their interest, for example, to rob other people as the preferred means of making a living. As a practical example today, we could say that drug dealers live as ethical egoists because they consider the money they make from drugs to be in their self-interest without regard for the ruinous consequences their actions bring upon their customers. The consequences of egoism are equally apparent in the newsroom example. While we live with the myth of the reporter as the independent, enterprising (and perhaps even crusading) lone wolf, in reality the reporter operates in a news-gathering environment that depends on teamwork and cooperation, and where following one's self-interest without compromise may ultimately be counterproductive. Two reporters at the same newspaper vying to interview the same source, and each operating as an ethical egoist, could undermine each other to the point where neither gets the interview. In this instance self-interest would work not only against the reporters themselves but also against the interest of their news outlet, which now has no story, and against the interest of their audience, which must go without the information the story would have conveyed.

Philosophers point out another problem with egoism: It cannot be advocated as a philosophy without contradiction. If I advocate egoism, I am telling you that you should pursue your self-interest even at the expense of mine. Clearly it is not in my self-interest to tell others to put their interests ahead of mine. The underlying assumption is that self-interests are mutually exclusive. That may or may not be so in every situation, but the literature on ethical egoism seems less willing than books on pop psychology and business management to admit the possibility of the so-called "win-win" situation. In contemporary terms the egoist is a member of the "me generation," and his goal in life is "looking out for Number One."

If the weaknesses of egoism are easily recognized and that approach discredited, it is quite a bit harder, on the face of it, to find fault with utilitarianism. After all, an altruistic theory that seeks to bring about the greatest good for the greatest number of people—regardless of oneself—would seem to be more worthy from an ethical perspective. Utilitarianism, however, does not travel without its own baggage.

The most common objection to utilitarianism is that it requires us to make predictions about what will happen in the future. That is, if we evaluate an action by its consequences we are making an assumption about how it will turn out at some point down the road. But we can never know with absolute certainty what the outcome will be in advance. If we don't know the outcome with certainty, how can we act with certainty? Because it is impossible to know exactly the outcome of an action, or of one outcome compared with the outcomes of other possible actions, it is impossible to know with certainty how to act.

Another objection is that utilitarianism focuses on consequences rather than on actions themselves. Thus, actions that produce morally desirable consequences could themselves be undesirable in moral terms. Utilitarianism (and particularly act utilitarianism) could condone murder, mayhem, genocide, and all other manner of horrific actions if the consequences yielded the greatest good for the greatest number.

The answer to these objections, at least in part, is rule utilitarianism. By following rules based on past experience, this method avoids the problem of having to predict the future. One tries instead to act according to rules that have yielded desirable outcomes in the past. The problem with rule utilitarianism, however, is that it tolerates injustice. A person may act in perfect accord with rule utilitarianism but still be acting without regard for just conduct. An example by Merrill and Odell illustrates this distinction:

> Suppose that there exist two fathers each of whom has five children. Suppose that one of them gives each of his children five dollars a week and that the other father gives his favorite child twenty-five dollars a week and gives his other children nothing.
>
> Suppose further that it just happens to be the case that the total pleasure that the five children of the former father

receive is exactly equivalent to the pleasure that the one child of the latter father receives. Also suppose that the other children of the second father are unaware that their sibling is being favored, and so do not experience any pain. Suppose further that each of these fathers acts in terms of a rule. The first father adopts the rule that each of his children is to get an equal share of what he can afford as allowance money. The second father adopts the rule that his favored child should receive all the money that he can afford to give.

All of us are inclined, are we not, to judge that the second father is unethical and that the first father has behaved in an exemplary way. Yet each of their rules is on equal footing with respect to the utilitarian maxim. Each rule produces the same balance of pleasure over pain. What this shows is, according to most philosophers, that ethics cannot be founded solely upon the principle of utility.[10]

Rule utilitarianism also suffers in its own way from the unpredictability of human existence. "Can rule or rules be found that in all cases will maximize the good?" asks ethicist Edmund Lambeth.[11] But even if rules are qualified, or made conditional to meet certain situations, "the flux and sometimes vexing variety of human experience make rules difficult to apply in all cases without compromise, without failing, in short, to maximize the good."[12] Can we fare any better if we look beyond teleological theories of ethics?

Deontological Theories of Ethics

The other major category of classical ethical theory is known as deontology, and it encompasses a rather broad range of theories that gained prominence in the 17th and 18th centuries and continued to modern times. Theories that do not focus primarily on the consequences of actions (as do teleological theories) but instead are concerned with the nature of the actions themselves are deontological. One can hardly address the topic of deontology without discussing Immanuel Kant, the 18th-century German philosopher whose books *Critique of Pure Reason* and *Critique of Practical Reason* are still seminal.

---

[10]Merrill and Odell, p. 82.

[11]Edmund B. Lambeth, *Committed Journalism: An Ethic for the Profession*, 2d ed. (Bloomington: Indiana University Press, 1992), p. 20.

[12]Ibid.

Kant's Categorical Imperative

According to Kant, an action is good if it is performed out of a sense of duty—a far different concept than acting out of self-interest or to achieve good consequences. This desire to act as one ought to act stems from what Kant would call a "good will" or a "right will," a rational will that is motivated by this sense of duty to do the right thing. How can one recognize the right thing to do? Kant's test of an action's moral goodness was his "categorical imperative": "Act only according to that maxim by which you can at the same time will that it should become a universal law."[13] We might paraphrase this by saying, "Choose to act in a way that would be good if everyone acted this way in every situation."

Criticisms of Kant's approach focus on the fact that the categorical imperative seems to work best in cases involving speech as opposed to actions; that it would consider too many actions morally wrong if they couldn't be universalized (e.g., if I decide that I want to become an astronaut, is that decision morally wrong if I can't universalize it by saying that everyone should become an astronaut?); and that it tells us when we are acting immorally (i.e., when the maxim cannot be met) but isn't clear about when we *are* acting morally (i.e., it doesn't distinguish adequately between actions that are morally good and morally neutral).

Kant can be said to be a "pure rule deontologist"—someone who judges the morality of an action according to a rule. Deontologists also come in the "pure act" variety:

> Such a person has been characterized as highly intuitive, spontaneous, and even "creative" in the way he reasons in morally demanding situations. To an act deontologist, no two circumstances are alike. Each is unique, so unique that the invocation of firm rules or codes is not possible. Not only is it not possible, it may actively prevent the doing of the right thing under the circumstances. The "right thing under the circumstances" must be what a diligent human, after searching consideration, *feels* to be the right thing to do. Thus, the act deontologist must consult one's innate ethical sense, one's inborn inertial guidance system.[14]

---

[13]Immanuel Kant, *Foundations of the Metaphysics of Morals*, translated by L. W. Beck (New York: Liberal Arts Press, 1959), p. 39, quoted in Merrill and Odell, pp. 85–86.

[14]Lambeth, p. 18 (emphasis in original).

Let us turn our attention to several contemporary schools of thought that reflect this approach.

Emotivism

This theory holds that many of the terms we use to characterize actions are not actually describing an objective reality about the action but are merely expressing our feelings about the action. Thus, the emotivist would contend that if I say, "The city manager was wrong to award those contracts to his brother-in-law," all I am really saying is, "I feel that action was wrong and I disapprove of it." Emotivism makes no claim that the action itself is inherently right or wrong, only that the action produces a feeling about its rightness or wrongness in the observer.

Emotivism makes a distinction between terms like "good," "bad," "right," "wrong," "beautiful," "horrible," and "sublime," which it calls "expressive," and another group of terms it calls "descriptive." Those are words that describe the objective reality of an object, such as its size, color, or other physical characteristics, and which can be verified by experience (e.g., measuring the object). Expressive terms are held to be subjective in nature, while descriptive terms are considered objective. I may express the feeling that this sports car is stylish, and you may find it unattractive. These are both subjective judgments, and neither one is more true than the other; both feelings can be said to be equally true or valid. However, if I say the car is red and you say it is blue, only one of us can be making a true statement (assuming the car *is* either red or blue). In this case, we are making descriptive statements about the car, the truth or falsity of which can be determined by observing the actual color of the finish. Emotivists hold that all values are equal because values are expressive concepts, subjective in nature, and thus unable to be proven right or wrong. In the realm of journalism, emotivists would caution that much of what reporters mistakenly regard as objective reporting is nothing more than a listing of a reporter's subjective feelings of approval or disapproval about what he or she is reporting.

Situationism

Another form of relativism, situationism, is practiced by many journalists although they may be unaware that their practical approach has a philosophical name. The situationist is mindful of ethical principles but, like the act utilitarian, believes that principles or rules are too abstract to offer enough guidance in specific situations. The situationist looks to the circumstances at hand to determine the correct course of action. That may mean making an exception to an ethical rule, but because no rule can cover every situation, the situationist is not disturbed by such exceptions. According to Merrill and Barney

> The journalistic situationist may well be the one who believes that he should tell the truth *as a basic principle*, or that he should not generally distort his story, but who will, after due consideration of the situation in which he finds himself, conclude that it is all right to distort *this particular story*, or even to lie. . . . He is a relativist to be sure, but a rational relativist, one who *thinks* before breaking a basic ethical rule.[15]

Existentialism

One of the most popular philosophical theories of the 20th century is existentialism as pioneered by French philosopher Jean-Paul Sartre. Existentialism can be said to have two main premises: reason is illusory, and God does not exist. Needless to say, such premises open up a lot of ethical maneuvering room. If God does not exist, there is no higher authority to consult as an arbiter of morals and values. Thus, man must decide for himself what is right and what is wrong, and one opinion will carry the same weight as the next. As in emotivism, existential value judgments are personal and subjective and cannot be proven false; therefore all are equally true.

What about appealing to reason as a guide to morally correct action? The existentialist dismisses such an approach, claiming that man's reasoning power is vastly overrated and is unable to fathom questions about the "big picture" of man's existence in the world and the universe. Kant's categorical imperative goes out the existentialist's window, depending as it does on the concept of a rational will that is able to reason through to a correct moral action. Out too goes utilitarianism, the approach that employs reason to deduce the consequences of potential actions.

Critics would contend that existentialism is synonymous with "anything goes." Followers of Sartre would prefer to see it as having a great liberating effect on human behavior. Existentialism makes

---

[15]John C. Merrill and Ralph D. Barney, eds., *Ethics and the Press: Readings in Mass Media Morality* (New York: Hastings House, 1975), p. 14 (emphasis in original).

it possible for you, if we can borrow the advertising slogan of the U.S. Army, to "be all that you can be." (Would an existentialist appreciate the paradox here—that the Army nurtures self-fulfillment within a framework of rules, discipline, and order, and even makes government-paid chaplains available to all its members? Somehow we doubt it.)

Existentialism is based on the concept that "existence precedes essence." That is, man came into being by accident, not because God created man in His image (essence preceding existence in human form). Thus, man is free to define his own essence as he proceeds through life, and the choices he makes (none of which is any better or worse than another) are a part of this self-definition. Every person possesses his or her own moral compass and is not bound by rule or reason in making moral judgments.

At first glance, that would not appear to be a very good prescription for journalists to follow, since it would seem to place a premium on personal subjectivity while minimizing the role of reason as a means of ascertaining the truth. And yet the application of existentialism to journalism did find expression in the 1970s, primarily in the writings of Merrill. Existential journalism, he wrote, is "mainly manifested in an attitude of freedom, commitment, rebellion, and responsibility . . . a *subjective* journalism, subjective in the sense that it puts special stress on the *person* of the journalist himself" (although it should be tempered with "reasonableness," he added). Merrill summarized the main features of the existentialist approach to journalism as follows:

- Takes a certain viewpoint, a certain position, a certain stand, and ceases what may be called the "objective-neutralism" fallacy;
- Considers alternatives of action and makes a commitment to one or some;
- Makes no hesitation in choosing, selecting, making decisions as to editorial determinations;
- Considers consequences of journalistic action and takes responsibility for it. . . . (The journalist *is his own standard*; there is no other);
- Accepts and *uses* freedom—personal and journalistic;
- Is vital, dynamic, passionate, and committed;
- Extols individualism.[16]

[16]Merrill, pp. 53–54 (emphasis in original).

One could easily say that this approach makes journalism primarily a means of self-fulfillment (or self-indulgence) for the journalist rather than a means of informing the public, seeking truth, or any of the other functions traditionally ascribed to the art of reporting. Existential journalism would seem to be a variation on the so-called New Journalism, the trendy 1970s deconstruction of traditional journalistic values. Not so, says Merrill. Although they have some characteristics in common, New Journalism is more concerned with form and style, an anti-establishment bias, and shocking the sensibilities of the public. By conforming to those goals, even though the goals are nonconformist, the New Journalist differs from the existential journalist who conforms to nothing in his quest to create his own "journalistic essence."[17]

Not surprisingly, perhaps, working journalists were not quick to embrace the principles of existential journalism. In fact, most of them couldn't figure out what Merrill was talking about. "I've never heard of it, I haven't got the time to look it up, and I doubt whether it has anything to do with the real world of writing and editing—or the teaching thereof," was the fairly typical reaction of one editor at the time.[18]

The Next Step: Ethical Principles

Classical ethical theory is the fundamental—though often overlooked or unrecognized—basis for the development of ethical principles. To the extent that journalists consciously reflect on their decisions at all, however, their highest level of reflection probably centers on ethical principles rather than on the ethical theories that underlie them. It is the unusual journalist indeed who would ponder a decision as follows: "Well, let's see. I have to decide whether I should include these facts about Smith's unsavory business dealings five years ago in this story about his mayoral campaign. He's far more qualified to be mayor than his opponent, and his economic recovery plan would be more beneficial to the city. But if I mention his business dealings in the interest of telling the whole story, I might damage his campaign and let his poorly qualified opponent win. Shall I approach this as an act utilitarian and decide in a way that

[17]Ibid., p. 54.
[18]Ibid., p. 26.

23

will have the best consequences for the people of the city; or should I look strictly at the moral nature of my decision (as a rule deontologist) and see if my decision stands up as a maxim that everyone should follow; or should I be a situationist and allow that I would normally include such facts, except in this particular case? Of course if I do that I'm practically being an act utilitarian anyway, and that theory *does* have some weaknesses."

Newsrooms are hardly the places of such reflection, and it is doubtful that any newspaper or newscast would meet its deadline if they were. Journalistic decisions are made quickly and on the basis of many considerations from the lofty to the mundane. Will this story angle get me in trouble with the editor? Is this the way other reporters have played this story before? Am I being true to the journalistic principle of truth telling? Is it worth missing my dinner reservations to stay late and follow up this lead?

Of these examples the noblest, of course, is the one dealing with truth telling. And this is an ethical principle, as opposed to an ethical theory. Truth telling in itself is not an ethical theory but rather a principle that can be justified by a number of ethical theories (the rule deontology of Kant's categorical imperative, for example, or rule utilitarianism that would say that telling the truth has proved by experience to bring the greatest good to the greatest number of people). When journalists reflect, they reflect on principles. When they act without reflecting, they are acting on the basis of principles they have already internalized, or according to the conventions of their news organization—conventions that are based on the principles the organization has adopted formally or informally.

Principles, then, can be thought of as "applied ethics," or as the means of converting ethical theory into a workable system of decisionmaking. Meaningful ethical principles cannot be developed without reference to the teleological and deontological theories of ethics we have examined, and that is the reason we have taken some time to outline them. Likewise, journalists cannot be expected to make sound and morally correct judgments under deadline pressure on the basis of ethical theory alone, but they *can* be expected to benefit immensely from a system of principles that implements ethical theory. (A system of principles should not be confused with a code of ethics, which is merely an attempt to formalize a system of principles in writing. Principles can and do exist without being written down as codes, becoming instead a part of a news organization's oral tradition or reflected in written operating procedures.)

If principles are the indispensable link between ethical theory and journalistic practice, how do we go about developing such principles? First, let us be clear about what we mean. When we speak of "principles," we will be limiting that term only to maxims or general rules based on philosophical theory. A newsroom can be a place of many rules, but not all rules have the stature of journalistic principles. Rules against smoking or conducting office football pools, for instance, could apply to many types of workers besides journalists. Other rules, such as those prohibiting workplace discrimination or sexual harassment, may have a basis in law quite apart from any moral imperative. Still other rules peculiar to the practice of journalism may be more in the nature of conventions, having some practical value but lacking a basis in philosophical theory. For example, using a tape recorder or taking detailed notes during an interview, and maintaining extensive files of tapes and notes, may have more to do with defending against potential libel suits than with the principle of truth telling.

Just as all rules are not principles, all principles are not based on ethical theory. Some principles, in fact, may be derived from other branches of philosophy such as epistemology. Discussions about the role of the press in a free society have much to do with our state of knowledge about the nature of man, the nature of freedom, the suitability of various forms of governance, and the interplay between governing and governed—political philosophy, if you will.

The classical liberalism of Thomas Jefferson, John Stuart Mill, and others gave us the theoretical framework that shapes our fundamental concept of the press to this day. Under this model, the press is privately owned and is left alone by government so that the press can both pursue the truth without interference and serve as a check on the actions of government. This approach embraces the "marketplace of ideas," the concept that good journalism and bad, truthful and untruthful, fair and unfair can all coexist without government control, and that the reader (or viewer) has the ability to choose from this selection that which is good, truthful, and fair. The truth will flourish not because government controls the flow of information (or even influences it indirectly by setting parameters for "appropriate" or "responsible" reporting), but because rational individuals can use their powers of reason to pick out the truth amid

25

the cacophony of competing ideas in the journalistic marketplace. Perhaps the strongest and most universal ethical principles that journalists have derived from classical liberal theory address the need for independence in news gathering and skepticism toward government. If independence is compromised, the first casualty is the truth; if independence is compromised in the face of government—either by government interference in journalistic structures and processes or by reporters' lack of skepticism toward government action generally—the casualty is the very system in which a free press functions as a check on government power.

Classical liberalism was challenged at midcentury by a theory that stressed journalism's responsibility to society and suggested a role for government in making sure the press performed appropriately. This approach, which came to be known as the "social responsibility" theory of the press, was outlined in 1947 in the report of the Commission on Freedom of the Press. The commission was headed by Robert M. Hutchins, a scholar with philosophical leanings "who was an outspoken advocate of certain classical (his detractors would say medieval) political, ethical, and educational ideals."[19]

The social responsibility theory goes something like this: "Freedom is a right enjoyed by the press. In exchange for the ability to speak freely, the press incurs an obligation to act responsibly in society." The next question, of course, is "What does it mean to act responsibly?" The Hutchins Commission (as it was popularly known) thought a responsible press was one that sought to meet certain needs of society; the commission translated those needs into a functional analysis of what the press should provide:

> first, a truthful, comprehensive, and intelligent account of the day's events in a context which gives them meaning; second, a forum for the exchange of comment and criticism; third, a means of projecting the opinions and attitudes of the groups in the society to one another; fourth, a method of presenting and clarifying the goals and values of the society; and fifth, a way of reaching every member of the society by the currents of information, thought, and feeling which the press supplies.[20]

[19]Newman, p. 113.

[20]Robert D. Leigh, ed., *A Free and Responsible Press: Re Freedom of the Press* (Chicago: University of Chicago Press,

As the points above show, the Hutchins Commission placed a premium on the responsibility of the press to function as society's educator—not only to educate one about the day's events but also about a range of commentary and criticism, other groups in society, and the very goals and values of society itself. That is a pretty tall order for any one institution, and the Hutchins Commission came in for its share of criticism for being too "scholarly and abstractional," "high-minded," and run by "Platonic elitists."[21]

But what chiefly concerned journalists—and libertarians—was the commission's belief that government ought to play a role in encouraging and ensuring a responsible press. "We recommend that government facilitate new ventures in the communications industry, that it foster the introduction of new techniques, that it maintain competition among large units through the antitrust laws, but that those laws be sparingly used," the commission said.[22] The thought that government ought to play *any* role in encouraging press responsibility met with harsh and immediate criticism from publishers and editors—who seemed largely unconcerned that the FCC had been regulating radio content (including news) for years and was already tightening its regulatory grip on the nascent television broadcasting industry.

Despite this, the Hutchins Commission report did have some points to recommend it. It drew heavily on the libertarian concept of the "marketplace of ideas," seeing the press as perhaps society's premier marketplace for information about the events, opinions, attitudes, and values that define society. The report's five points on what a responsible press should do could be said to hearken back to the deontological concept of choosing to act according to principles out of a sense of duty or obligation—to "do the right thing." Still, the serious philosophical work of the commission was clouded by its belief that government should be an agent of press accountability. Although social responsibility has been the subject of much discussion in the last half century, it has not translated into a set of ethical principles per se. Lambeth has attributed this to the commission's failure to offer much "to the individual journalist or media

---

[21]Newman, pp. 25, 113, 143.
[22]Leigh, p. 83.

organization that could focus on a dialogue on ethics"[23]—perhaps because the commission's philosophy was primarily utilitarian, with its attendant weaknesses. Theodore Peterson, who articulated the social responsibility theory in the 1956 book *Four Theories of the Press*,[24] noted in 1981 that "the ethic that has developed is an unreasoned ethic without a philosophical base."[25]

Ethics Today

As our brief review has attempted to show, journalistic ethics are the product of many competing forces, many of which are not related to ethics at all. News organizations develop "ethical standards" that may or may not be based on principles; those principles may be derived from ethical theory, from another branch of classical philosophy, or from political philosophy. More likely these "ethical standards" are based on little more than common sense, or what has worked well before, or an intuitive sense about journalistic values, or newsroom conventions about what makes a good story. (They may also be legalistic responses to government regulations or practices, but that is the subject of the next chapter.) Journalists generally do not know how to approach the subject of ethics from a philosophical perspective and tend to be wary of the philosophers who do. Philosophers, on the other hand, can become so bogged down in abstractions and philosophical minutiae that they are of little practical help to journalists.

In any event, a field as diverse as journalism that deals in a commodity as broad as speech may not be well served by a single ethical approach or a universal code of ethics. Still, it would be nice to perceive a sense of direction, an "ethical highway" that most journalists recognize as the main route for getting from here to there in an ethical sense, with plenty of byways, side roads, and detours for those so inclined.

The beginnings of one such highway are suggested by two publications: Lambeth's *Committed Journalism*, which first appeared in 1986 and is now in a second edition; and *Doing Ethics in Journalism*, a

---

[23]Lambeth, p. 8.

[24]Fred S. Siebert, Theodore Peterson, and Wilbur Schramm, *Four Theories of the Press* (Urbana: University of Illinois Press, 1956).

[25]Quoted in H. Eugene Goodwin, *Groping for Ethics in Journalism*, 2d ed. (Ames: Iowa State University Press, 1987), p. 8.

looseleaf handbook for journalists published in 1993 by the Society of Professional Journalists and its Sigma Delta Chi Foundation.

Lambeth recognizes the need for a system of ethical *principles*— something more than a collection of common sense, newsroom folklore, and conventions. Such a system, he says, should possess several characteristics: It should "embody the values of Judeo-Christian and classical Greek civilizations," reflecting the values of the larger society; "reflect working principles" that journalists can apply, and provide a means of resolving conflicts among them; be flexible, yet "yield similar decisions when applied by different individuals in similar circumstances"; be mindful of the teleological and deontological approaches of classical ethical theory; and finally, be a system that "journalists themselves find fair and useful" and that provides "a basis for criticism and corrective reflection."[26]

Lambeth recommends a framework that incorporates "mixed-rule deontology." This approach places primary emphasis on acting according to rules or principles but also allows some consideration of consequences, recognizing that an action is not disembodied from its consequences. He enumerates five ethical principles that should guide journalists: (1) the principle of truth telling; (2) the principle of justice; (3) the principle of freedom; (4) the principle of humaneness; and (5) the principle of stewardship.[27]

Lambeth's five principles can be thought of as a set of "rules of just conduct" for journalists. *Truth telling* encompasses the striving for factual accuracy and authenticity. It also implies an obligation to raise one's journalistic competence to the highest level by learning the language of one's sources, be it statistics, econometrics, computer programming, or whatever: "Without one or more of these skills he or she may come far less close to the truth in his or her work, may fail to realize his or her potential as a moral agent, as a truth teller."[28]

Justice, on one level, is premised on treating one's sources and readers with an abiding sense of fairness. On a deeper level, the principle of justice exhorts the journalist to monitor how well the Constitution's promise to establish justice and promote the general welfare is, in fact, being carried out by society's major social, political,

---

[26]Lambeth, pp. 23–24.
[27]Ibid., pp. 24–32.
[28]Ibid., p. 26.

and economic institutions. How the journalist assesses the performance of these institutions depends in large measure, of course, on how the journalist conceives of justice. But Lambeth is silent on this point. If one sees justice in terms of promoting, in a positive sense, the "general welfare," then one could have journalists justifying a welfare state and massive redistribution. If, on the other hand, one envisions justice in the classical-liberal sense of protecting individual liberties (including property rights and freedom of speech), then one could have journalists justifying limited government. Lambeth's vagueness implies a tolerance for various concepts of justice (including misguided ones), provided they are well intentioned.

Freedom carries two implications: (1) the obligation to safeguard the First Amendment and the freedom of the press it guarantees and (2) the need to remain autonomous and independent, that is, free from coercion by sources. *Humaneness* refers to what John Rawls has called "the natural duties":[29] doing no direct, intentional harm to others; preventing harm where possible; and rendering assistance to fellow human beings when needed. *Stewardship* operates on multiple levels: being a steward of one's own talents; a steward of the institution of journalism; a steward of free expression. Journalist-stewards manage communication resources "with due regard for the rights of others, the rights of the public, and the moral health of their own occupation."[30]

Doing Ethics in Journalism is a practical attempt to do much of what Lambeth recommends. It is light on theory and heavy on case studies, but it does outline the difference between teleological and deontological concepts (without mentioning them by name). Like Lambeth, the authors arrive at a mixed-rule deontology but distill it into only three rather than five "guiding principles for the journalist": (1) seek truth and report it as fully as possible; (2) act independently; and (3) minimize harm.[31] Point one corresponds directly to Lambeth's first point about truth telling; to "act independently" corresponds to Lambeth's principle of freedom and also incorporates

---

[29]Ibid., p. 30, citing John Rawls, *A Theory of Justice* (Cambridge, Mass.: Harvard University Press, 1971), pp. 114–17.

[30]Ibid., p. 32.

[31]Jay Black, Bob Steele, and Ralph Barney, *Doing Ethics in Journalism: A Handbook With Case Studies* (Greencastle, Ind.: Sigma Delta Chi Foundation and Society of Professional Journalists, 1993), p. 11.

his principle of stewardship; and to "minimize harm" mirrors his principle of humaneness.[32]

Two factors make this handbook significant: It is an attempt to develop an ethical system of principles based on classical ethical theory that appears to recognize Lambeth's excellent work in this regard, and it is published by SPJ. If this does not make it an "official" publication for journalists, it should at least increase the odds that journalists take it seriously.

Summary

Ethics is one of the liveliest topics of debate in journalism today. The development of ethical standards is a dynamic, creative process, changing in response to external forces, yet grounded (one hopes) in ethical theory. Lapses in journalistic performance like the *Dateline NBC* segment on exploding pickup trucks, however, give evidence to a skeptical public that journalists have no ethics, or that the standards of the craft are so low as to be meaningless. But standards clearly do exist and are the product of much discussion among serious journalists and academicians. Whether those standards are consistently embraced by particular news organizations or individual journalists is another matter, of course. One would have to conclude, for example, that the producers of that *Dateline* segment fell short in meeting SPJ's principles of seeking the truth and reporting it as fully as possible, and of minimizing harm. They were following conventions for "good TV," perhaps, but those are not the same as ethical standards. And the producers could fall back on the rationale that they had done nothing illegal.

That last point is telling because it suggests the problems that arise when ethical standards are confused with legal standards, and when following laws or government regulations is confused with acting ethically. The dynamic process of ethical development among

[32]Black, Steele, Barney, and Lambeth are not the only ones, of course, who have articulated sets of journalistic principles. See, for example, Stephen Klaidman and Tom L. Beauchamp, *The Virtuous Journalist* (New York: Oxford University Press, 1987). Their chapter titles enumerate seven broad principles: "reaching for truth"; "avoiding bias"; "avoiding harm"; "serving the public"; "maintaining trust"; "escaping manipulation"; and "inviting criticism and being accountable." At the working level, the American Society of Newspaper Editors set forth a "statement of principles" that lists six: "responsibility"; "freedom of the press"; "independence"; "truth and accuracy"; "impartiality"; and "fair play."

journalists and academicians is being threatened more and more by the hand of government that, directly and indirectly, has been imposing its own set of "ethics" on the practice of journalism—especially in the electronic media. That is a foreboding development, at odds with both the concept of a free press and with the very ethical standards that thoughtful journalists have been developing. We call this the substitution of government ethics for private ethics, and we shall address it in the next chapter.

3. The Substitution of Government Ethics for Private Ethics

The process of making ethical decisions is a complex one, as we have seen. Editorial decisions are often made not on the basis of principles rooted in classical ethical theory or even political theory, but on the basis of newsroom conventions, how things have been done before, and intuition. Commercial factors (i.e., the need to report in a way that attracts a large audience for advertisers) play a major role. But a less-discussed factor in journalists' decisionmaking has been the influence of government.

Journalists (and especially those in the electronic media) have been subjected to myriad government regulations, many of which affect the content of programming. The Communications Act of 1934 prohibits the FCC from engaging in program censorship or interfering with free speech[1]—but the FCC has regulated content since its earliest days and continues to do so today in a host of ways, both subtle and blatant. The ostensible ban on content controls recognizes that the federal government grants radio and television broadcasters limited First Amendment rights and that outright content control is a form of censorship that infringes on even those limited rights.

Broadcasters' First Amendment rights are limited because Congress still prefers to believe the airwaves are a scarce resource that government must regulate as trustee of the public interest. But communications attorney and media consultant Ford Rowan, who observed the situation firsthand as an NBC reporter in the 1980s, sees the situation for what it is:

> It's not so much that the airwaves are scarce, but that they have become enormously valuable and the allocation of frequency is a grant of power—something that directly affects politicians no matter where they stand on the political spectrum.[2]

[1]See *Communications Act of 1934*, 47 U.S.C. Sec. 326 (1988).

[2]Ford Rowan, *Broadcast Fairness: Doctrine, Practice, Prospects* (New York: Longman for the Media Institute, 1984), p. 39.

33

Historically the Fairness Doctrine was perhaps the most blatant example of government interference in the editorial process despite the prohibition on content controls. Other examples affecting both news and entertainment are plentiful, however, including rules on political editorializing, personal attacks, licensing requirements (which judge an applicant's mix of programming content), prime-time access, and children's programming. (The Children's Television Act of 1990 is probably the most blatant content-specific legislation on the books today.) Nor are print journalists immune to government meddling. Court decisions have weakened journalists' claims to confidentiality; reporters have become easy targets for invasion-of-privacy actions; and the libel law process has become so convoluted that even a journalist's state of mind enjoys prominent legal stature.

The difficulty, then, is that journalists (electronic and print) end up making more and more decisions not because of a desire to follow ethical standards of their own choosing (private sector or "private" ethics) but because they must comply with government regulations and fear the consequences if they don't. We call those mandates "government ethics"; even though they are not ethics at all, they function as de facto ethical standards because they strongly influence journalists' decisions and compete with legitimate (private) ethical standards for journalists' attention. All things being equal, however, a journalist will usually substitute the government ethic for the private ethic because noncompliance with the former is a much harsher proposition. Therefore, there is no real decisionmaking to be done. Fear of government sanctions dictates the journalist's action, short-circuiting the ethical decisionmaking process and rendering moot any authentic ethical debate.

And thus we have a system wherein decisions are increasingly made according to law rather than ethics—and the two are not the same. Ethics is the process of moral decisionmaking, of moral choice. It exhorts us to do the right thing because doing so is virtuous and right in itself (as Kant might say). Ethics strives for the ideal.

Law, on the other hand, is imposed on the individual from the outside; it is not developed internally. Nor is it a matter of moral choice in the same way. One may choose to act legally or illegally, and one may choose to act ethically or unethically. In the former case, choosing to act legally is motivated by fear—the desire to avoid punishment. Choosing to act ethically, however, is motivated by virtue—the desire to strive for a moral ideal. To put it another way, when one acts legally one is choosing not to fall below a certain minimum standard of conduct. When one acts ethically one is choosing to act according to the highest standard of conduct.

The authors of SPJ's *Doing Ethics in Journalism* note this distinction:

> Ethical constraints are not the same as legal rules. . . . There is a common tendency today to equate ethical standards with legal standards, and for victims of unethical behavior to seek legal remedies for perceived ethical lapses. This is a false equation and a fundamental misconception of the relationship between law and ethics. For instance, invasion-of-privacy laws widely permit the publication of information that, for reasons of ethics, taste, compassion, or professionalism, some news media would not publish or broadcast.[3]

The substitution of government ethics (laws and regulations) for private ethics, then, has a debilitating effect on the ethical process. It moves the ethical perspective downward, from striving for the highest good to meeting a minimum standard. And it makes this downward shift mandatory by imposing penalties on those who fail to comply. No government agency has pursued this substitution of government ethics for private ethics more aggressively than the FCC.

A Legacy of Control

A look at FCC history may open the eyes of those who are surprised that the FCC still acts in accordance with the scarcity rationale; seems eager to embrace "reregulation" in the wake of the Fowler, Patrick, and Sikes deregulatory regimes; and continues to act as if electronic media were invented to be regulated.

As we noted earlier, the Communications Act of 1934 prohibits the FCC from interfering in program content. The Radio Act of 1927, which preceded it, did likewise. But in 1928 the Federal Radio Commission told Congress that "the Commission believes it is entitled to consider the program service rendered by the various applicants, to compare them, and to favor those which render the best

---

[3]Jay Black, Bob Steele, and Ralph Barney, *Doing Ethics in Journalism: A Handbook With Case Studies* (Greencastle, Ind.: Sigma Delta Chi Foundation and Society of Professional Journalists, 1993), p. 8.

service."[4] By 1929 the FRC had developed standards for program service that would be used to judge how well applicants served the "public interest, convenience and necessity." According to the FRC, "the tastes, needs and desires of all substantial groups among the listening public" would be met by a "well-rounded" mix of programming composed of

> entertainment, consisting of music of both classical and lighter grades, religion, education and instruction, important public events, discussion of public questions, weather, market reports, and news and matters of interest to all members of the family.[5]

By the mid-1940s the commission's power to deny new license applications and renewals on the basis of program content was unchallenged. So pervasive was its power that the commission (now the FCC) flouted the legislative ban on content control in its public documents. A 1946 report titled *Public Service Responsibility of Broadcast Licensees* stated:

> The contention has at times been made that Section 326 of the Communications Act, which prohibits censorship or interference with free speech by the Commission, precludes any concern on the part of the Commission with the program service of licensees. This contention overlooks the legislative history of the Radio Act of 1927, the consistent administrative practice of the Federal Radio Commission, the re-enactment of identical provisions in the Communications Act of 1934 with full knowledge by the Congress that the language covered a Commission concern with program service, the relevant court decisions, and this Commission's concern with program service since 1934.[6]

It should be clear, the FCC concluded in its defense, "not only that the Commission has the authority to concern itself with program

---

[4]FRC, *Annual Report to Congress for 1928*, p. 161, quoted in FCC, *Public Service Responsibility of Broadcast Licensees* (Washington: Government Printing Office, 1946), p. 10.

[5]Great Lakes Broadcasting Co., reported in FRC, *Third Annual Report*, pp. 33–35, quoted in FCC, *Public Service Responsibility of Broadcast Licensees*, p. 10.

[6]FCC, *Public Service Responsibility of Broadcast Licensees*, p. 9.

service, but that it is under an affirmative duty, in its public interest determinations, to give full consideration to program service."[7]

And so it did. By the 1940s, the FCC was concerned about broadcasters' attempts to substitute sponsored programming for what was then known as "sustaining" programming—shows that were not paid for by advertisers and did not contain commercials. Licensees were expected to broadcast a good deal of such programming and to make "sustaining" time available to religious, civic, agricultural, labor, and educational groups in fulfillment of a station's "public interest" requirement. The commission was also concerned that stations were cramming too many commercials into their schedules. The FCC warned licensees that it was cracking down and told them exactly what it expected in terms of program content:

> The Commission proposes to give particular consideration to four program service factors relevant to the public interest. These are: (1) the carrying of sustaining programs, including network sustaining programs, with particular reference to the retention by licensees of a proper discretion and responsibility for maintaining a well-balanced program structure; (2) the carrying of local live programs; (3) the carrying of programs devoted to the discussion of public issues, and (4) the elimination of advertising excesses.[8]

New applicants not proposing to comply with the FCC's content regulations would have no hope of winning a license; existing licensees would face a tough time upon renewal and could lose their license altogether.

The FCC's interest in dictating government ethics to broadcasters became even more pronounced during the activist years of the Kennedy administration. In his famous "vast wasteland" speech to the National Association of Broadcasters in 1961, FCC chairman Newton Minow unleashed his wrath on the broadcasting industry:

> When television is bad, nothing is worse.... I can assure you that you will observe a vast wasteland. You will see a procession of game shows, violence, audience participation shows, formula comedies about totally unbelievable families,

[7]Ibid., p. 12.
[8]Ibid., p. 55.

blood and thunder, mayhem, violence, sadism, murder, western badmen, western good men, private eyes, gangsters, more violence, and cartoons. And endlessly, commercials—many screaming, cajoling, and offending. And most of all, boredom. . . .
In the past licenses were often renewed *pro forma*. I say to you now: renewal will not be *pro forma* in the future. There is nothing permanent or sacred about a broadcast license.[9]

A year later the FCC formalized Minow's ideas about good taste in television in a document titled *En Banc Programming Inquiry Report and Statement of Policy.*[10] A major imposition of government ethics on private broadcasters, the statement told licensees that they had better broadcast a schedule of programming having specific characteristics and types of shows if they hoped to retain their licenses:

(1) opportunity for local self-expression, (2) the development and use of local talent, (3) programs for children, (4) religious programs, (5) educational programs, (6) public affairs programs, (7) editorialization by licensees, (8) political broadcasts, (9) agricultural programs, (10) news programs, (11) weather and market reports, (12) sports programs, (13) service to minority groups, (14) entertainment programs.[11]

Many of the FCC's content controls became more subtle as the years went on, but the regulatory mindset persisted.[12] With some limited exceptions during the Reagan and Bush years, one could say that the commission's regulatory philosophy has changed little since 1928 when the old FRC proclaimed:

Listeners are given no protection unless it is given to them by this Commission, for they are powerless to prevent the

---

[9]Quoted in Jonathan W. Emord, *Freedom, Technology, and the First Amendment* (San Francisco: Pacific Research Institute for Public Policy, 1991), p. 198.

[10]FCC, *En Banc Programming Inquiry Report and Statement of Policy,* 44 F.C.C. 2303 (1962).

[11]Ibid. at 2314.

[12]During the Reagan and Bush years (1981–92) chairmen Fowler, Patrick, and Sikes tried to move the FCC in the direction of deregulation by getting rid of some outdated regulations, reducing reporting requirements, and dabbling in lotteries and auctions for the allocation of certain spectrum rights. However, the FCC stopped far short of embracing any fundamental change in its historical role as regulator of a public trust. In the Clinton era, the pendulum seemed to be swinging back toward "reregulation" and a pronounced role for government in creating the "information superhighway."

ether waves carrying the unwelcome messages from entering
the walls of their homes.[13]

The Fairness Doctrine

No single regulation sums up the FCC's interest in regulating
program content more dramatically than the Fairness Doctrine. First
defined in the FCC's *Report on Editorializing by Broadcast Licensees* in
1949, the Fairness Doctrine required broadcasters to present coverage of controversial issues of public importance in their communities
and to provide reasonable opportunities for the expression of con-
trasting viewpoints on those issues.[14] The rationale for this doctrine
was twofold: (1) the obligation of the broadcaster to act in the public
interest, convenience, and necessity and (2) the right of the public
to be informed:[15]

> The paramount and controlling consideration is the relation-
> ship between the American system of broadcasting carried
> on through a large number of private licensees upon whom
> devolves the responsibility for the selection and presentation
> of program material, and the congressional mandate that
> this licensee responsibility is to be exercised in the interests
> of, and as a trustee for the public at large which retains
> ultimate control over the channels of radio and television
> communications. . . .
>
> And we have recognized . . . the paramount right of the
> public in a free society to be informed and to have presented
> to it for acceptance or rejection the different attitudes and
> viewpoints concerning these vital and often controversial
> issues. . . . It is this right of the public to be informed . . .

---

[13]Quoted in FCC, *Public Service Responsibility of Broadcast Licensees*, p. 41.

[14]FCC, *Report on Editorializing by Broadcast Licensees*, 13 F.C.C. 1246, 1249 (1949).

[15]The right to receive information had become firmly embedded in First Amendment
jurisprudence by the 1960s and 1970s. See, for example, the Supreme Court's decisions
in *Lamont v. Postmaster General*, 381 U.S. 301, 305 (1965) (First Amendment rights of
citizens to receive political publications from abroad); *Kleindienst v. Mandel*, 408 U.S.
753, 762–763 (1972) (right to "receive information and ideas"); *Procunier v. Martinez*,
416 U.S. 396, 408–409 (1974) (censorship of prisoners' mail infringes First Amendment
rights of recipients); and *Va. State Board of Pharmacy v. Va. Consumer Council, Inc.*, 425
U.S. 748, 762–764 (1976) (right of consumers to receive price information through
advertising).

which is the foundation stone of the American system of broadcasting.[16]

The Supreme Court affirmed both of these rationales in its 1969 *Red Lion* decision, which addressed the Fairness Doctrine's corollary rules on personal attacks and political editorializing (which we shall discuss later). The Court enshrined the concept that broadcasters are entitled to less First Amendment protection than print media or other speakers when it stated, "It is the right of the viewers and listeners, not the right of the broadcasters, which is paramount."[17]

Critics continued to maintain that the doctrine actually had the counterproductive effect of chilling discussion of controversial issues. A broadcaster would find it preferable to avoid airing stories on controversial topics altogether rather than go to the time and expense of defending against a Fairness Doctrine complaint. Those who continued to cover controversial topics could avoid expense only by relinquishing their freedom as speakers in determining the speech reaching their audiences. As Jonathan Emord has noted, "Broadcasters came to accept that the principal Fairness Doctrine complainants were well-financed special interest groups, which, regardless of the legal merit of their challenges, would file complaints knowing that the cost of defense alone could be enough to force the broadcasters to provide the groups with free air time."[18]

Despite mounting criticism, the FCC of the mid-1970s stood by *Red Lion*:

> The problem of scarcity is still very much with us. . . . Far from inhibiting debate, however, we believe that the doctrine has done much to expand and enrich it. . . . In the years since *Red Lion* was decided, we have seen no credible evidence that our policies have in fact had "the net effect of reducing rather than enhancing the volume and quality of coverage."[19]

But in a stunning about-face a decade later, the Reagan-era commission acknowledged the chilling effect of the doctrine. The FCC's 1985 report on the Fairness Doctrine took a marketplace approach

---

[16]FCC, *Report on Editorializing by Broadcast Licensees*, 1247, 1249.

[17]*Red Lion Broadcasting Co., Inc. v. FCC*, 395 U.S. 367, 390 (1969).

[18]Emord, *Freedom, Technology, and the First Amendment* p. 239.

[19]FCC, *Fairness Report*, 48 F.C.C. 2d 6, 7, 8 (1974).

to viewpoint diversity, gave greater recognition to the First Amendment rights of broadcasters, and concluded that the Fairness Doctrine was, in fact, counterproductive:

> We find that the fairness doctrine, in operation, actually inhibits the presentation of controversial issues of public importance to the detriment of the public and in degradation of the editorial prerogatives of broadcast journalists.[20]

Still, the FCC continued to enforce the Fairness Doctrine, even though the commission itself had shot down the scarcity rationale and recognized the doctrine's constitutional shortcomings.

Two court cases in the 1980s proved pivotal in determining that the Fairness Doctrine could be abolished. In 1986, *Telecommunications Research and Action Center v. FCC (TRAC)* addressed the issue of whether the Fairness Doctrine's political broadcasting corollaries applied to the new medium of teletext. Judge Robert Bork's larger consideration, however, was whether the Fairness Doctrine itself was mandated by statute or merely an "administrative construction" of the FCC. Fairness Doctrine proponents claimed that it was mandated by law, citing a 1959 amendment to section 215 of the Communications Act that prevented certain types of newscasts, interviews, and spot coverage from triggering fairness requirements for political broadcasting. But the amendment also stated that it did not relieve broadcasters of their obligation "to operate in the public interest and to afford reasonable opportunity for the presentation of conflicting views on issues of public importance."[21] Judge Bork held that the 1959 amendment did not codify the Fairness Doctrine, but merely ratified the FCC's long-standing policy:

> The language, by its plain import, neither creates nor imposes any obligation, but seeks to make it clear that the statutory amendment does not affect the fairness doctrine obligation as the Commission had previously applied it.[22]

---

[20]FCC, *General Fairness Doctrine Obligations of Broadcast Licensees*, 102 F.C.C. 2d 147 (1985)—commonly referred to as the 1985 Fairness Report.

[21]*Communications Act of 1934*, 47 U.S.C. Sec. 315(a) (1988). See also Pub. L. No. 86–274, 73 Stat. 557 (1959).

[22]*Telecommunications Research and Action Center v. FCC*, 801 F.2d 501, 517 (D.C. Cir. 1986).

A year later, the D.C. Circuit Court of Appeals ruled in *Syracuse Peace Council v. FCC* that the commission could indeed abolish the Fairness Doctrine:

> We conclude that the FCC's decision that the fairness doctrine no longer served the public interest was neither arbitrary, capricious nor an abuse of discretion, and are convinced that it would have acted on that finding to terminate the doctrine even in the absence of its belief that the doctrine was no longer constitutional. Accordingly we uphold the Commission without reaching the constitutional issues.[23]

But the Fairness Doctrine refused to die. Members of Congress, fearing their access to the airwaves would be jeopardized without a fairness mandate, sought to codify the doctrine into law. President Reagan vetoed one such attempt to amend the Communications Act, and similar provisions tacked on to budget bills were dropped under threat of veto by President Bush. Oddsmakers were betting that a fairness bill would have smooth sailing in the Clinton administration, but that has not been the case at this writing.[24] Action stalled on a bill introduced by Reps. John D. Dingell (D-Mich.) and Edward J. Markey (D-Mass.) in part because of grassroots opposition generated by Rush Limbaugh and other talk show hosts, who feared that a revived Fairness Doctrine would be used to stifle their critiques of government. Back in the courts, the FCC's repeal of the doctrine was upheld again in December 1993 by the Eighth Circuit Court of Appeals in a drawn-out case that had pitted a Little Rock TV station against the AFL-CIO.

In June 1994, President Clinton did everything except call for an immediate reinstatement of the Fairness Doctrine as he lashed out at what he called talk radio's "constant, unremitting drumbeat of negativism and cynicism." Calling in to a St. Louis radio show, the president noted with frustration that "Rush Limbaugh will have three hours to say whatever he wants, and I won't have any opportunity to respond, and there is no truth detector."[25] The Fairness Doctrine may be dormant at present, but no one is claiming that a wooden stake has been driven through its heart once and for all.

[23]*Syracuse Peace Council v. FCC*, 867 F.2d 654, 669 (D.C. Cir. 1989).

[24]J. Laurent Scharff, "Still on Track," *Communicator*, February 1994, p. 9.

[25]Douglas Jehl, "Clinton Calls Show to Assail Press, Falwell and Limbaugh," *New York Times*, June 25, 1994, p. A1. See also "Excerpts From Clinton's Comments on Cynicism and the Press," ibid., p. A12.

Corollary Rules on Political Broadcasting

One of the prerogatives of the airwaves' government overseers is the ability to impose ethical standards on broadcasters that favor politicians' own political interests. Such is the case with a number of codified FCC rules dealing specifically with how broadcasters are to treat candidates for office (including incumbents). They are the political editorializing rule, personal attack rule, and the equal opportunities rule.[26]

The political editorializing rule requires licensees who editorialize for or against political candidates to notify the opponents of the candidate being endorsed, or the candidate being opposed, and provide an opportunity to respond using the licensee's facility.

The personal attack rule covers a variety of attacks on a person's honesty, character, or integrity that can arise during discussions of controversial issues of public importance. The licensee must notify the person so impugned and provide access for the person to reply. The rule specifically exempts candidates who are bashing each other, but it does apply to the editorials of licensees—and presumably affords access to politicians who might be criticized by the broadcaster.

The equal opportunities rule requires a broadcaster who makes time available to one candidate to make time available to other candidates for that office. A broadcaster abusing this provision can have its license revoked. Moreover, the rule states that candidates must be offered time at the lowest unit rate charged to commercial advertisers and that "stations shall not establish a separate, premium-period class of time sold only to candidates."[27] The legislators who passed this provision were, in effect, telling broadcasters, "When we run for reelection you have to give us airtime if you give our opponents airtime, or if you attack us in an editorial (even though we are public figures), or if your editorials merely oppose our reelection. You have to sell us time at your cheapest rates,

---

[26]Strictly speaking, the equal opportunities rule is not a corollary to the FCC's Fairness Doctrine but is a congressional mandate codified at 47 U.S.C. Sec. 315 (1988). It is discussed in this section because it is philosophically identical to the Fairness Doctrine and subject to the same constitutional arguments against content-based controls over the broadcast industry. See also *Personal Attacks*, 47 C.F.R. Sec. 73.1920 (1992) and *Political Editorials*, 47 C.F.R. Sec. 73.1930 (1992).

[27]*Candidate Rates*, 47 C.F.R. Sec. 73.1942(a)(1)(vi) (1993).

give us the same deals and discounts you give your commercial advertisers, and we specifically forbid you to charge us premium rates—no matter how much that time is worth to us."

Jonathan Emord notes that these corollaries are several of the "regulatory and statutory rights that members of Congress had long used to attain political objectives and to gain access to broadcasting":

> For more than fifty years the FCC had kowtowed to political pressure from Congress and had used the Fairness Doctrine and the political programming rules as part of the government's overall effort to require broadcast licensees to satisfy an often partisan conception of balanced journalism. . . . [The doctrine and rules] had become favorite tools of Congress and special interest groups in their struggle to prevent broadcasters from having free reign over programming.[28]

Interestingly enough, the rules protecting politicians' access to the airwaves are still in effect even though the Fairness Doctrine itself has been repealed. Although the doctrine has been found to disserve the public interest and to be constitutionally infirm, its corollaries remain in force despite the same weaknesses—a tribute to the power of broadcasting's congressional masters.

Other Content Controls on Broadcasters

The Fairness Doctrine and political broadcasting rules may be the most blatant example of the substitution of government ethics for private ethics in the broadcasting realm, but they are certainly not the only ones. Over the years the FCC has imposed dozens of rules that have taken ethical decisionmaking out of the hands of broadcasters. The following are but a few examples of FCC regulations and requirements that have imposed this substitution of ethics.

Licensing Requirements

The FCC approves or denies license applications and renewals by passing judgment on the applicant's "citizenship, character, and financial, technical, and other qualifications."[29] This approach is based on the scarcity rationale, as if the community owns the airwaves and asks the FCC to find the most qualified manager for a

---

[28]Emord, pp. 240–41.
[29]47 U.S.C. Sec. 308(b) (1988).

particular slice of spectrum. In recent years, the FCC has also given preference to minority ownership and local ownership. The commission's 1978 *Statement of Policy on Minority Ownership of Broadcasting Facilities*, for example, allows broadcasters facing license revocation to transfer or assign their licenses to applicants with a "significant minority ownership interest" at "distress sale" prices.[30] One of the assumptions of such licensing requirements and preferences is that different types of applicants will choose different types of programming than other applicants, thereby leading to greater program diversity. Until recently, applicants were required to present detailed predictions about the type and amount of programming they planned to carry, and those predictions were used both as a basis for awarding a license and as a standard against which to measure actual performance at renewal time. As a court noted in a 1931 license renewal case, "In considering an application for a renewal of the license, an important consideration is the past conduct of the applicant, for 'by their fruits shall ye know them.' Matt. VII:20."[31]

Licensing requirements present a twofold problem, however: Applicants design their applications around what the FCC prefers in terms of structure and programming (thereby substituting government standards for private ones); and there is no guarantee that the FCC's selection of applicants with particular characteristics will actually yield certain programming or predictable performance overall.

In the 1980s, the commission stopped comparing licensees' predictions with their actual performance and instead instituted a "meritorious programming" standard that judged an applicant's performance by five criteria:

1. The licensee's efforts to ascertain the needs, problems, and interests of its community;
2. The licensee's programmatic response to those ascertained needs;
3. The licensee's reputation in the community for serving the needs, problems, and interests of the community;

---

[30]FCC, *Statement of Policy on Minority Ownership of Broadcasting Facilities*, 68 F.C.C. 2d 979, 983 (1978).

[31]*KFKB Broadcasting Association v. FRC*, 47 F.2d 670, 672 (D.C. Cir. 1931).

4. The licensee's record of compliance with the Communications Act and FCC rules and policies; and
5. The presence or absence of any special effort at community outreach or toward providing a forum for local self-expression.[32]

Nonetheless, the process remained highly subjective and still resulted in renewals being awarded to those who conformed to "government ethics."

Ownership Rules

The FCC attempts to promote viewpoint diversity by ensuring ownership diversity. Until recently, a broadcaster could not own two of the same types of stations in the same community, nor can a newspaper and broadcast outlet in the same area share the same ownership (cross-ownership restrictions). National concentration of ownership is also restricted; an individual or company may own no more than 12 AM, 12 FM, and 12 television stations nationwide. Such ownership restrictions are premised on the scarcity rationale; concentration of ownership would lead to a monopoly on viewpoints in a scarce environment, the thinking goes. But, by denying individuals a chance to operate certain outlets or in certain cities, the commission denies those individuals the very opportunity to act ethically (i.e., to make ethically based decisions about how a media outlet should be operated to meet the public interest). Fearful that media operators will act unethically if given the chance, the FCC bars them (through ownership restrictions) from having the chance to act at all.

Other Rules

The FCC imposes many other rules on broadcasters that, while not dealing with journalists per se, have ethical overtones nonetheless. Indecent material, which would be protected by the First Amendment in print media, is subject to criminal penalties. ("Whoever utters any obscene, indecent, or profane language by means of radio communication shall be fined not more than $10,000 or imprisoned

---

[32]Quoted in Emord, pp. 214–15.

not more than two years, or both."[33]) The FCC has also told broadcasters that they must familiarize themselves with the lyrics of records they play so as not to encourage drug use.[34]

Over the years the FCC has imposed content-related restrictions on almost every conceivable topic: astrological information, horse races, certain contests and promotions, betting advertisements, foreign-language programs, and alcoholic beverage ads to name but a few.[35] The Reagan-era commission eliminated those and other "nuisance" restrictions on broadcasters, but too many still remain and more can be anticipated in the "reregulatory" atmosphere of the Clinton era.[36]

In the broadcasting realm, the substitution of government ethics for private ethics is felt most acutely in decisions about program content. Most government content regulations are justified by the scarcity rationale—but that rationale was discredited by the FCC itself in its 1985 Fairness Report, and by Judge Bork in *TRAC*.[37] Television and radio journalists are generally thought to lag behind print journalists in the contemplation and formulation of ethical standards. While this no doubt stems from a number of factors, one cannot be overemphasized: Government's pervasive regulation of the broadcasting industry has preempted the ethical debate, resulting in the substitution of "government ethics" for private ethics. If broadcasters are constantly told what they must do, there is less reason for them to contemplate what they *should* do.

Legal Restraints on Journalists

While the electronic media alone bear the brunt of FCC regulations, the ethical debate for both electronic and print journalists is

[33]18 U.S.C. Sec. 1464 (1988). See also *FCC v. Pacifica Foundation*, 438 U.S. 726 (1978).

[34]See FCC, *Licensee Responsibility to Review Records Before Their Broadcast*, 28 F.C.C. 2d 409 (1971). See also dissent of Justice Douglas in *Yale Broadcasting Co. v. FCC, cert. denied*, 414 U.S. 914 (1973).

[35]Emord, pp. 234–35.

[36]The broadcast television industry is bracing itself for new content regulations. On April 20, 1994, the FCC scheduled a hearing seeking comments on the "quantity and quality" of children's television programming. The FCC will consider what programming is most edifying for children and how often it must be broadcast. See Kim McAvoy, "Kids' TV Moves Up on FCC Agenda," *Broadcasting & Cable*, April 25, 1994, p. 6.

[37]See FCC, *General Fairness Doctrine Obligations*, pp. 196–98, and *TRAC*, 801 F.2d at 508–509.

shaped to a large extent by the body of law that has grown up primarily in two areas: invasion of privacy and defamation. The problem, from an ethical standpoint, is that both are ethical issues. Violating another individual's privacy and damaging another's reputation orally (slander) or in writing (libel) are actions that touch on basic ethical principles of humaneness and justice. Ethical debate on these topics can easily become clouded when ethical considerations are overlaid with a body of law that may confuse, contradict, or even ignore a journalist's ethical ruminations. This situation has the same characteristics as broadcast regulation: "Government ethics" prescribe minimum standards of acceptable conduct rather than advocate the highest or noblest behavior; and, because failure to comply with the government's standards can have harsh consequences, journalists can be forgiven if they are naturally inclined to substitute a reliance on legal standards for a reliance on ethical standards. Meanwhile, individuals who feel they have been wronged by the media seek legal remedies for what may often be more properly considered ethical violations. The issue is further clouded by the "freedom of the press" argument. While reporters have enjoyed certain privileges and immunities in the course of their work, the courts have never interpreted "freedom of the press" to mean the unchecked freedom to invade the privacy or defame the reputations of others.

Invasion of Privacy

Journalists are subject to tort actions in four broad categories involving privacy: intrusion, private facts, false light, and commercialization. Intrusion includes actions such as taping phone conversations without the subject's knowledge or consent; trespassing; engaging in surreptitious surveillance; and obtaining information under false pretenses. Intrusion generally hinges on the reporter's conduct during the news-gathering process, rather than on publication of information.

Private facts (also known as "intimacy") claims arise when a media outlet publishes or broadcasts details about an individual's private life that a reasonable person would find offensive, and that are not of legitimate interest to the public. The traditional defense is not truth, but newsworthiness: If the private facts are newsworthy, courts will generally uphold their public airing. (In this instance the courts have legalized a utilitarian ethic, i.e., informing the public at the expense of one individual's privacy is thought to yield the greatest good for the greatest number of people.)

"False light" refers to publicizing an individual in a manner that places him or her in a false light before the public, provided that a reasonable person would find the false light offensive and that the journalist knew the publicized material was false or acted in reckless disregard as to its falsity. False light is similar to defamation, but false light claims generally seek compensation for emotional distress or injury to one's feelings, as opposed to damage to one's reputation.

Commercialization claims, the fourth category of privacy torts, tend to involve the appropriation of persons' names and images without their consent for advertising or commercial purposes. Such claims are likely to be of more concern to publishers than to working journalists.

Libel Law

It would not be stretching too far to say that the courts, rather than any journalistic codes or principles, have been the major factor influencing journalists' decisions regarding libel. The concept of redress for damage to one's reputation has a long history in common law, predating the press as we have known it in this country's lifetime. Publishers originally faced a standard of strict liability; if a plaintiff's name was damaged, even because of an oversight or innocent mistake, the publisher was liable. Eventually publishers were granted certain privileges that required a plaintiff to show the publisher had violated the privilege or had acted out of ill will. "At common law, what was important was whether someone was hurt, not who they were or how or why they were hurt."[38]

That situation changed dramatically in 1964 with the Supreme Court's decision in *New York Times Co. v. Sullivan.*[39] That ruling gave journalists a constitutional privilege, based on the First Amendment, that tolerated the publication of some falsehood as an almost unavoidable by-product of debate that was "uninhibited, robust, and wide

---

[38]Randall P. Bezanson, Gilbert Cranberg, and John Soloski, *Libel Law and the Press: Myth and Reality* (New York: Macmillan, 1987), p. 2.

[39]*New York Times Co. v. Sullivan*, 376 U.S. 254 (1964).

open."[40] Moreover, the case established the concept of "actual malice" with respect to public officials. That is, a public official bringing a libel action now had to prove that the publisher had known the material was false, or had reason to suspect it was false, and had printed it anyway with reckless disregard for what he knew or suspected about its falsity.

In 1967, the Court extended the actual malice standard to "public figures" as well as public officials in *Curtis Publishing Co. v. Butts.*[41] A year later, the Court said that liability required proof that a publisher "in fact entertained serious doubts as to the truth of his publication."[42] And in 1974, the Court referred to a publisher's "subjective awareness of probable falsity" in *Gertz v. Robert Welch, Inc.*[43] Central to the actual malice standard in all of these cases is what came to be known as the journalist's "state of mind"—what he or she thought to be the truthfulness of the material. The Court defended this approach in its 1979 verdict in *Herbert v. Lando*:

> Reliance upon such state-of-mind evidence is by no means a recent development arising from *New York Times* and similar cases. Rather, it is deeply rooted in the common-law rule, predating the First Amendment, that a showing of malice on the part of the defendant permitted plaintiffs to receive punitive or enhanced damages.[44]

By the 1980s it was clear that libel law was in a state of disarray. Epic cases like *Westmoreland v. CBS, Inc., Tavoulareas v. Washington Post Co.*, and *Sharon v. Time, Inc.* drew public attention to the fact that major libel actions consumed thousands of hours and millions of dollars yet were not guaranteed to yield clear-cut winners and losers. The picture was even bleaker for defendants of more modest means. In Illinois, the *Alton Telegraph* was forced into bankruptcy in the face of a $9.2 million award of punitive damages against it.[45] It is impossible to calculate the chilling effect of large punitive damage awards on the editorial (and ethical) decisions of journalists.

[40]Ibid. at 270.
[41]*Curtis Publishing Co. v. Butts*, 388 U.S. 130 (1967).
[42]*St. Amant v. Thompson*, 390 U.S. 727 (1968).
[43]*Gertz v. Robert Welch, Inc.*, 418 U.S. 323 (1974).
[44]*Herbert v. Lando*, 441 U.S. 153, 161–162 (1979).
[45]*Green v. Alton Telegraph*, 8 Med. L. Rep. (BNA) 1345 (Ill. App. Ct. 1982).

In courtrooms around the country, the theoretical framework of libel jurisprudence was being supplanted by a patchwork of categorical rules, a situation exacerbated by *Gertz v. Robert Welch, Inc.*[46] Bezanson et al. note the daunting task that judges have come to face in libel cases:

> Distinctions must first be adjudicated on the basis of the plaintiff's identity as a public official, public figure, private person, or public or private entity. For those cases involving private plaintiffs, the identity of the defendant as media or non-media must be ascertained, an inquiry which involves not only the breadth and purposes of the statement's distribution, but also an assessment of the public significance of the statement in light of that distribution. These steps determine the level of privilege applicable to the case. Thereafter, the privilege itself must be adjudicated in terms of either actual malice or negligence, with attendant issues relating, for example, to scope of discovery and availability of evidence.[47]

The discovery process has become yet another example of government intrusion into the decisionmaking processes of journalists. The actual malice standard, with its emphasis on the journalist's state of mind, has turned discovery into a thriving cottage industry.[48] Every sheet of notes, every story draft, every bit of scribbling in a reporter's desk might shed some light on his state of mind and so become fair game for the plaintiff's attorneys. A reporter's decisions about what to keep and what to discard are now effectively made by government; the prudent media attorney will counsel the reporter to keep everything just in case. Competing with the ethical decision-making process, then, is the de facto requirement to go about the

---

[46]*Gertz v. Welch* expanded upon the privileges set forth in *Sullivan*, resulting in a more complex and structured set of constitutional privileges. But as Bezanson et al. note, the *Gertz* rules suffer from "the absence of a clear and sensible theoretical relationship between the rules and the constitutional policies being served by the privileges," p. 203.

[47]Bezanson et al., p. 200.

[48]The Supreme Court rejected the argument that allowing the government to gain access to confidential sources and notes would impede news gathering and held that the First Amendment contains no privilege against compelled release of confidential sources in a criminal case. *Branzburg v. Hayes*, 408 U.S. 665 (1972). Reporters are given slightly more protection in civil suits except, as a practical matter, when defending libel cases.

news-gathering process as if one is constantly preparing to defend against a libel action. A reporter not only has the ethical obligation to write the truth but now has the legal obligation of documenting to judge and jury that he *believed* it was the truth at the time he wrote it. The Supreme Court in *Herbert* recognized the added burden on reporters:

> In every or almost every case, the plaintiff must focus on the editorial process and prove a false publication attended by some degree of culpability on the part of the publisher. If plaintiffs in consequence now resort to more discovery, it would not be surprising; and it would follow that the costs and other burdens of this kind of litigation would escalate and become much more troublesome for both plaintiffs and defendants.[49]

The Court observed that "deposition-discovery rules are to be accorded a broad and liberal treatment," and in the next breath reminded district court judges that they should use their powers "to exercise appropriate control over the discovery process."[50] Apparently *Herbert* was an example of the rules' being given "broad and liberal treatment"; the Court noted that CBS producer Lando's deposition continued intermittently for over a year, filling 26 volumes containing nearly 3,000 pages and 240 exhibits.[51]

By the early 1980s, libel law had become so confused and burdensome that it began to attract the serious attention of academicians and legal scholars interested in improving the dispute resolution process. One noteworthy venture in this regard was the Iowa Libel Research Project, a multidisciplinary endeavor conducted under the auspices of the University of Iowa. The project conducted an extensive survey of participants in libel actions and emerged with four principal conclusions about the motivations and actions surrounding libel litigation:

1. The dominant interest expressed by libel plaintiffs is the correction of falsity, or setting the record straight. Plaintiffs' interest in the libel process, therefore, is focused on the question of truth or falsity.

[49]*Herbert*, 441 U.S. at 176.
[50]Ibid. at 178.
[51]Ibid. at n.25.

2. The interaction between media and plaintiffs, following publication, often fosters rather than discourages litigation. This may be the most important single factor explaining the large number of "petty" claims that ripen into lawsuits.
3. The issue of truth or falsity of the challenged statement is rarely adjudicated in the lawsuit. Instead, privilege issues dominate adjudication of virtually all claims, including many of those that are successful.
4. Most plaintiffs win by suing; they do not sue only to win in court. Plaintiffs sue to correct falsity, to deter republication, and to get even. The act of suit, itself, represents the only available form of self-help through which plaintiffs' claims of falsity can be legitimized and vindicated.[52]

The litigation process could hardly do a poorer job of meeting the plaintiffs' needs identified by the Iowa group, and its findings sparked a movement for libel law reform. That movement has taken several turns: In 1987, the Iowa project undertook an experimental Libel Dispute Resolution Program in cooperation with the American Arbitration Association. The program employed arbitration-style proceedings to adjudicate issues of reputational harm and the truth or falsity of the challenged statements. Malice, negligence, and reporters' state of mind were irrelevant, and discovery on those points was prohibited. Remedies were nonmonetary, usually consisting of publication or broadcast of a finding of falsity. What proved to be a stumbling block, however, was the requirement that participants agree to waive further legal action. An additional problem was that plaintiffs' attorneys, often working for contingency fees, had little incentive to seek a nonmonetary remedy once they had begun the litigation process.[53]

On another front at that time, a distinguished group of attorneys and constitutional scholars was developing a proposal for the reform

---

[52]Bezanson et al., p. 182.

[53]Conversation with John Soloski, August 4, 1994. See John Soloski and Roselle L. Wissler, "The Libel Dispute Resolution Program: A Way to Resolve Disputes out of Court," in *Beyond the Courtroom: Alternatives for Resolving Press Disputes*, Richard T. Kaplar, ed. (Washington: Media Institute, 1991).

of libel law. Working under the auspices of the Annenberg Washington Program in Communications Policy Studies of Northwestern University, the group recommended legislation that would (1) provide initially for retraction or right of reply, (2) offer the option of declaratory judgment to determine the truth or falsity of the challenged statements, and (3) provide an action for money damages, limited to actual damages only; punitive damages would be barred.[54]

This and other proposals for legislative reform faced a rocky road. What emerged from those efforts by early 1994 was the "Uniform Correction or Clarification of Defamation Act" developed by the Conference of Commissioners on Uniform Laws. Approved by the American Bar Association, the act is the scaled-down product of a three-year attempt to draft a Uniform Defamation Act. It provides a mechanism for the timely correction of false statements, but still allows plaintiffs to recover punitive damages if certain conditions are met. The uniform statute awaits adoption by the 50 state legislatures.[55] Clearly, it is not a wholesale reform of libel law; moreover, the specter of punitive damages still looms large, exerting its chilling effect on the editorial process.

Government's Chilling Effect on Private Initiatives

Thus far, this chapter has looked at ways in which government compels journalists to act in response to regulations and laws. The TV broadcaster who airs a local show in the prime-time access slot and the newspaper reporter who keeps extensive files of old interview notes may or may not be acting out of an ethical concern—but they are unquestionably responding to "government ethics" that mandate certain behaviors on their part if they wish to avoid time-consuming and costly legal entanglements.

Government ethics also play a more insidious role by influencing journalists' decisions in areas where the government has no direct involvement. This is a "chilling effect" plain and simple, springing from the realization that government is already extending its grasp to areas that heretofore have been a part of journalism's private domain. This is especially true in the realm of news councils and

[54]See Richard M. Schmidt Jr., "A Proposal for Libel Law Reform," in *Beyond the Courtroom*.

[55]Lee J. Levine and Daniel M. Waggoner, "The Uniform Correction or Clarification of Defamation Act: Overview of the Act," *Communications Lawyer*, Winter 1994, p. 8.

codes of ethics where the journalistic craft makes some attempt at self-policing and self-correction.

News Councils

The Republic's sole attempt at a voluntary, national body to review and investigate press complaints led a short and largely unhappy life between 1973 and 1984. The National News Council was conceived as a forum to give voice to the average citizen who was unhappy with some aspect of media performance. The council limited its scope to national media—the TV networks, newsmagazines, and newspapers of national influence like the *New York Times* and *Washington Post*. During its lifetime the council received 1,253 complaints; it issued decisions on 227 and found against the media (fully or partially) in only 82 of the 227 decisions.[56] The council finally collapsed in 1984 under the weight of two problems that had vexed it since the day it opened its doors: an inability to attract broad-based funding in sufficient amounts and a lack of participation by media organizations. This lack of participation, in turn, had two causes. The first was simple independence—media outlets did not feel they needed a group of outsiders passing judgment on their performance. Because the council had no power to compel news organizations to participate in complaint investigations, or to abide by its determinations, or even to publicize its findings, it had little impact.

But there was another reason that at least some media outlets spurned the National News Council—they feared the council could, at some point, be grasped by the long arm of government, or at least foster an environment conducive to government regulation. When the News Council was announced in 1973, *New York Times* publisher Arthur O. Sulzberger sent his staff a memo outlining the *Times'* opposition to the new venture. Much of the memo's rationale could be viewed as editorial independence—participation would amount to "an unjustified confession that our own shortcomings are such that we need monitoring by a press council. . . . We do not wish anyone to impose standards on us."[57] But Sulzberger was also aware of the government threat:

---

[56]Louise W. Hermanson, "The National News Council Is Not a Dead Issue," in *Beyond the Courtroom*, p. 23.

[57]Patrick Brogan, *Spiked: The Short Life and Death of the National News Council* (New York: Priority Press Publications, 1985), pp. 118, 119.

> And while the Council as proposed is nongovernmental and
> would not have any enforcement powers beyond publication
> of its findings, we fear that it would encourage an atmosphere
> of regulation in which government intervention might gain
> public acceptance. This whole approach is dangerous, and
> we believe that we must resist it.[58]

His fears were not without basis. In 1981, lawyers for entertainer Wayne Newton demanded access to the council's records to prove that two NBC reporters had a history of subpar performance. Newton was suing NBC for libel over a story by the pair, who had also done an NBC story on oil issues that the council had found wanting. Prominent First Amendment attorney James Goodale helped the council fend off the incursion, but the bigger issue of confidentiality was still hanging when the council folded in 1984.[59]

The experience of a similar body in Great Britain gives no comfort to those who fear government intervention in private press councils. In 1953, Britain established the General Council of the Press, a voluntary, private group funded by the press itself. "It was Britain's answer to the problem of preserving the freedom of the press while at the same time trying to ensure its responsibility, and to resolve the grievances of those who felt they had been wronged," wrote its final chairman.[60] Yet in 1990, a government report recommended that the Press Council be abolished, to be replaced by a Press Complaints Commission—another voluntary body that would be the industry's last chance to police itself. And so it was done. The government report was clear that if this new commission failed to rein in the press, it would be replaced by a statutory commission having legal power over the press, or even by a statutory complaints tribunal—"a judge appointed by the Lord Chancellor sitting with two assessors appointed by the Home Secretary, ruling whether newspapers were in breach of a statutory code."[61] It could never happen here, we can say with confidence. But what about the administrative law judge appointed by the FCC chairman, ruling on a broadcaster's license

---

[58]Ibid., p. 119.

[59]Ibid., pp. 54–55.

[60]Kenneth Morgan, "The British Press Council Experience," in *Beyond the Courtroom*, p. 127.

[61]Ibid., p. 128.

renewal? And where will the line be drawn when newspaper companies deliver information electronically to one's television set?

The CBS Benjamin Report

Attempts by news organizations to critique their own performance likewise run the risk of being appropriated by government. Perhaps the best example of this is *The CBS Benjamin Report*.[62] In January 1982, CBS broadcast a documentary titled "The Uncounted Enemy: A Vietnam Deception," which charged that Gen. William C. Westmoreland had directed a conspiracy to "suppress and alter critical intelligence on the enemy." In late May, *TV Guide* ran a cover story by Don Kowet and Sally Bedell, "Anatomy of a Smear," which alleged CBS improprieties in preparing the documentary. CBS News president Van Gordon Sauter asked Burton Benjamin, a senior network news producer, to investigate *TV Guide's* charges. Benjamin submitted a 59-page written report to Sauter in July 1982, finding that the documentary had failed to prove its contention of a conspiracy and noting irregularities in the selection and "coddling" of sympathetic sources.

In the course of General Westmoreland's subsequent $120 million libel suit against CBS, his lawyers petitioned the court for release of the *Benjamin Report* as part of the discovery process. The U.S. District Court in Manhattan agreed, denying CBS's claim of First Amendment privilege. Thus, a candid document prepared by a veteran newsman to help a news organization identify and learn from its mistakes became part of the public domain.

Writing during the Westmoreland trial in 1983, media analyst (and former NBC correspondent) Robert Goralski grasped the implication of the court's order:

> It is most unlikely another such report will ever be written, for release of the *Benjamin Report* by a federal court over the objections of CBS will inhibit or even totally preclude further candid self-examinations of operational matters by television news organizations. Knowing that internal memoranda and documents could be released to the public, networks and local news staffs will not be disposed to commit to paper

---

[62]Burton Benjamin, *The CBS Benjamin Report: CBS Reports "The Uncounted Enemy: A Vietnam Deception," an Examination* (New York: Columbia Broadcasting System, 1982). Reprinted with an introduction by Robert Goralski (Washington: Media Institute, 1984).

possibly incriminating material revealing the motives and techniques of electronic news reporting, particularly documentaries.[63]

To the best of our knowledge, and more than a decade later, Goralski's prediction has not been disproved. If such self-criticism has indeed been stifled, so too has the process of ethical development. Ethical standards are born in part out of reflection upon real world experience; experience, in turn, is measured by ethical standards. We can only wonder how many opportunities for ethical growth have gone unrealized by the fear of government intervention in private attempts at self-examination.

Codes of Ethics

The debate over journalistic ethics inevitably turns to codes of conduct, their purpose, and their usefulness. Lately the government has been intervening in this journalistic venue as well, but that development may best be explored by putting codes in some ethical perspective. Codes of ethics are attempts by journalistic organizations to list the ethical standards that newsroom personnel are expected to follow. Somewhere in the neighborhood of 100 newspapers have their own codes, as do scores of electronic outlets. Professional organizations like the Society of Professional Journalists and the Radio-Television News Directors Association have also promulgated codes.

There is some agreement that codes have public relations value or, as editors prefer to phrase it, that codes enhance the credibility of news organizations with their audiences. The usefulness of codes beyond that is open to some debate. Those who believe journalists should make their own judgments based on broad ethical principles feel that codes can become lists of dos and don'ts that reporters will follow mechanically without contemplating the ethical questions involved; in that sense ethics codes can actually *retard* ethical growth, it is feared. In 1975, for example, the American Society of Newspaper Editors replaced its 1922 code of ethics with a broad "statement of principles" that stops short of detailed guidance. On the other hand, those who favor detailed codes recognize that even the most specific

[63]Ibid., p. v.

guidelines can never anticipate every situation, and must be constantly updated to accommodate changing conditions. (Former CBS news executive Emerson Stone even argues that standards should be rewritten or dropped entirely if a news organization no longer plans to heed them.)[64]

On a more philosophical plane, it is argued that a code of ethics is a sign of professional stature that journalism does not merit at all because, strictly speaking, journalism is more craft than profession (e.g., there are no competency or licensing requirements or disciplinary boards). And philosophers have a field day picking apart existing codes, citing their questionable assumptions about the role of journalism, abundant examples of faulty logic, imprecise language, and lack of connection to classical ethical theory.[65]

On top of all these concerns that are a part of authentic ethical debate, a new layer of concern has been overlaid: the legal implications of codes. No longer are journalistic codes of ethics something to be developed, followed, reworked, and generally debated within the confines of a private media industry. Government has begun to appropriate ethics codes for use in libel trials, allowing plaintiffs to introduce codes as "proof" that a journalist failed to meet professional standards. A court holding a journalist to an ethical standard (i.e., an ideal) instead of a legal standard (i.e., an acceptable minimum) represents the ultimate confusion of ethics and law. For example, a neurosurgeon in Denver reportedly won a $370,000 actual malice suit in which he claimed that the defendant, a weekly newspaper called *Westword*, had violated the SPJ code of ethics.[66]

A debate raged recently over a new ethics code developed by the Associated Press Managing Editors. It was a detailed code that included sections on accuracy, alteration of photos, alteration of quotes, conflicts of interest, fairness, honesty, promises, and the use of polls and surveys. Much of the debate focused not on the code's ethical dimensions, but on its legal implications. First Amendment attorney Richard Winfield, who represents Associated Press, opposed

---

[64]Emerson Stone, "Going, Going, Gone . . . ?" *Communicator*, December 1993, p. 16.

[65]See, for example, Chapter 2 in Jeffrey Olen, *Ethics in Journalism* (Englewood Cliffs, N.J.: Prentice-Hall, 1988).

[66]Alicia C. Shepard, "Legislating Ethics," *American Journalism Review*, January-February 1994, p. 41.

the code because its detailed guidelines on procedures such as fact checking could backfire in court:

> If a newspaper doesn't have a fact-checker or doesn't verify quotes for an article ... it gives the plaintiff's lawyer the opportunity to challenge the absence of a systematic verification and to show the newspaper violated the national standard set by a prominent and prestigious organization. Therefore, the newspaper has been at fault. Write your check. In the real world, that's how it works.[67]

Winfield's view prevailed, as the organization opted instead to revise its 1975 code of general guidelines.

The threat of government appropriation has rendered ethics codes less ethical than they might otherwise be. A code that is influenced by legal considerations is necessarily less influenced by purely ethical considerations. In practice, this means that codes can be left too vague to do much damage in court, can be tailored to reflect legal rather than ethical standards (on topics like privacy and libel, for instance), or can just not be written at all. Not having a code might seem to be the best way of avoiding government appropriation, of having a code used in court against the very people it is supposed to guide. Yet as Bezanson et al. point out, the lack of codes may merely make it easier for courts to substitute government ethics for private ethics:

> The journalism community plays, at best, a modest role in articulating meaningful principles of conduct and judgment. Increasingly, in large part out of a fear of liability, news organizations are unwilling to commit policies and procedures to writing as part of an effort to deny courts the raw materials with which to enforce the journalistic community's own standards. . . . Journalists are leaving courts and juries freer reign in developing their own standards by which conduct is to be judged in litigation.[68]

One can hardly think of a more unpalatable situation than a court's enforcing a news organization's ethical standards as if they were laws—except, perhaps, a situation in which a court enforces ethical

[67]Ibid. See also George Garneau, "In Defense of an Ethics Code," *Editor & Publisher*, April 9, 1994, p. 12.

[68]Bezanson et al., p. 199.

standards (government ethics) of its own creation. As we shall see in the next chapter, however, the substitution of government ethics for private ethics is not the only way—and maybe not even the most onerous way—in which government retards the development of ethical conduct in journalism.

4. Technology and Structural Impediments to Journalistic Ethics

The process of determining general principles of journalistic ethics, translating those principles into workable standards, and perhaps formalizing those standards in written codes is a dynamic though formidable undertaking as we saw in Chapter 1. That process is fraught with tensions ranging from honest debate of the principles themselves to questions of whether standards should be expressed as highly specific rules or general guidelines, to the temperamental differences between working journalists and philosopher academicians. Still, the process of ethics formulation and ethical decisionmaking forges ahead amid growing signs of cooperation between journalists and ethicists.

But, as we saw in Chapter 2, this process is complicated by the presence of government laws and regulations that have the effect of substituting "government ethics" for private ethics. Laws and regulations dictate minimum standards of performance and penalize those who do not meet the minimum. Ethical standards, on the other hand, exhort journalists to the highest levels of conduct demanded by the nature of the calling, yet do not offer incentives and rewards commensurate with the fines and punishments that accompany legal mandates. It is no wonder, then, that laws and regulations serve as disincentives to ethical decisionmaking. "Government ethics" having the force of law drive out private ethics and drive down ethical standards to the point of minimum acceptable conduct.

Yet, laws and regulations are not the only way, or even the worst way, in which government hinders the ethics process. In addition to these legal disincentives, the government has erected *structural* barriers to higher journalistic ethics by hindering the development of the very media in which ethical standards have a greater chance of flourishing.

If one were to condemn 200 journalists to life on a bus built for 50, few would argue that the perspectives and opinions of all on board would be deeply colored by their circumstances. To put it another way, one would immediately presume a connection between the medium and the message.

What is not seen as clearly is the connection between some of the new technologies of communication, on the one hand, and journalistic ethics on the other. But a connection does indeed exist. Perhaps we can illustrate this link between ethics and new technologies most clearly by looking at the old technologies. There is general agreement among media scholars and critics that major newspapers provide more news, and news of higher quality, than do the television broadcast networks. Much of the ethics debate, meanwhile, takes place between academicians and print journalists. No doubt this stems in large part from print journalism's First Amendment heritage and the ethical implications that flow from the concept of constitutionally protected speech. But the lack of full First Amendment protection for electronic media is no reason to suggest that journalistic ethics should be of less concern to broadcast news organizations. Ethics should be a priority, but unfortunately TV journalists are constrained not only by the government control we have already outlined but by the commercial and economic factors peculiar to broadcast television.

Television journalists are driven by the economics of a medium that demands a mass audience, which in turn is attracted by dishing up news that is graphic, entertaining, and at times sensational. These audience-grabbing standards dictate the TV journalist's conduct, and ethical standards are tolerated to the extent that they do not interfere with the commercial realities of "good television." Newspapers have their own commercial realities, of course, but are not faced with the same economic particulars; thus, newspapers have the luxury, as it were, of pursuing journalistic standards that are not overshadowed by commercial pressures to the same extent as in broadcasting. Some would say that the structure of the print medium is simply more conducive to ethical behavior.

Consider what could happen if an electronic medium were developed that did not face the extreme and overriding pressure to garner the largest possible audience at all cost. Such a medium might provide an environment in which journalists were free to refine their ethical sensibilities and pursue journalistic standards that were not overshadowed by commercial pressures; news organizations might become known for substance if not glitter and glitz. The electronic medium that has evolved along these lines to the greatest degree is the cable television industry. Yet, government stifled its early development and continues to thwart cable's expansion in a host of ways, thereby stifling an environment in which journalistic ethics have an opportunity to thrive. To appreciate this situation more fully, it is helpful to understand first just how radically cable differs from over-the-air broadcasting in terms of technology, economics, and programming.

Different Technologies, Different Economics

Television broadcasting is an "old" technology that gained commercial feasibility in the mid-1940s and popular acceptance by the early 1950s. A station, duly licensed by the federal government, uses a portion of the electromagnetic spectrum to broadcast a signal to a television receiver in the home. Originally, television reception was limited to 12 channels (2 through 13 in the very high frequency, or VHF, band). Channels 14 through 83, (constituting the ultrahigh frequency, or UHF, band), were the engine of growth for independent stations in the 1960s following passage of the All-Channel Receiver Act. (By 1970, the average TV home received 6.8 channels owing to the growing popularity of independent stations.)

When the FCC published its final frequency assignments in 1952, the 50 largest cities received at least two VHF station slots, but only 27 of those cities received more than two. That led to the development of only two television networks, because it was felt that a network, to be successful nationally, must reach at least the top 50 cities. CBS and NBC became the pioneers of network television, in part because they were able to capitalize on programming concepts and advertisers associated with their extensive and successful radio networks. Following the demise of the Dumont Network and the rise of the American Broadcasting Companies (ABC) in the 1950s, the network landscape remained unchanged until the advent of the Fox Network some 30 years later (1986).

It was during the 1970s that cable television began to gain prominence. Cable was originally known as "community antenna television," or CATV, and was a means of retransmitting broadcast signals to homes in rural areas. The coaxial cable that linked television sets to an operator's "head end" could carry multiple signals, however, and cable operators eventually took advantage of that capacity to create 12-channel systems that foreshadowed today's 60- and 120-channel systems. Unlike broadcasting, no scarcity rationale could be advanced as a reason for regulating the medium. Coaxial cable was not in short supply; from a technological standpoint, the only arguable limitation was the number of cables that would fit on a utility pole—and even then the wire could be buried underground. Still, the FCC managed to bring cable under its regulatory ambit, claiming that cable was an ancillary means of distributing broadcast signals. Meanwhile, municipalities established elaborate franchising procedures to ensure that no system would be built without substantial and ongoing remuneration to the local franchising authority. In 1980, the average TV home was receiving 9.8 channels, a number that had ballooned to 39.4 channels by 1993.

The economics of broadcasting and cable television differ significantly. Broadcasting depends on a single revenue stream—advertising. From an economic standpoint, broadcast networks do not exist primarily to entertain and inform viewers but to round up large numbers of consumers (preferably with certain demographic characteristics) and rent them to advertisers. The real clients of the networks are advertisers, not viewers. Broadcasters, in fact, have no way of knowing *precisely* who is watching at any given moment, and thus have no way of charging viewers. A single revenue stream (i.e., advertising dollars)—and a single channel—makes it incumbent upon networks to seek out maximum audience size at all times, because advertising rates are based on numbers of viewers. Thus, broadcast television depends upon mass audiences for its economic survival.

Cable, on the other hand, enjoys the benefits of a dual revenue stream—advertising dollars *and* subscriber revenues. For most of its history, cable depended virtually exclusively on the monthly subscription fees paid by viewers because cable audiences were too small to attract the attention of major advertisers. The advertising picture improved as cable viewership rose; in 1970, cable attracted only 4.5 million subscribers, compared with 61 million in 1993. Cable advertising revenues have been growing at the same time that broadcasting advertising revenues have been declining. Even though the absolute numbers are still heavily stacked toward broadcasting (about $28.1 billion per year compared with $3.6 billion per year for cable), the trend lines for ad revenues bode well for cable and ill for broadcasters.

A dual revenue stream is one reason that cable is not beholden, as broadcasting is, to the mass audience. The other is that cable is a multichannel medium that can target many channels of programming simultaneously to relatively small, subject-specific audiences. In this way, cable systems can operate profitably by pursuing a strategy of narrowcasting, or niche marketing, in which programming is financed by both advertising revenues and subscriber fees. And this difference in economic structure leads to a profound difference in the type of programming that each medium can offer, as we shall see.

Broadcast Programming: Commercial Pressures

Broadcasting's economic structure, as an advertiser-financed medium that viewers receive for free, made it inevitable that television would have to develop programming that appealed to the broadest spectrum of the public. It also meant that the potential of television to do more than merely entertain would go largely untapped. It is easy to forget that those who were present at the creation of television envisioned great things for this wondrous new medium. Its ability to bring news of current events from around the world and discussions of public affairs by national and world leaders into one's home was eagerly anticipated by many. TV pioneer Edward R. Murrow warned, however, that television could amount to much less:

> This instrument can teach, it can illuminate; yes, and it can even inspire. But it can do so only to the extent that humans are determined to use it to those ends. Otherwise it is merely wires and lights in a box.[1]

By the time Murrow intoned this oft-quoted remark in 1958, however, the economics of TV broadcasting had long since dictated the nature of program content. "He offered a critique laced with resignation and even bitterness. Murrow laid much of the blame for what he saw as television's failure to live up to its enormous potential at the feet of the very commercial interests that had long since made him rich," notes David Bartlett.[2] Yet, Murrow should not have been surprised. As long as broadcast TV had to aim programming at the

[1]Quoted in David Bartlett, "Landscaping the Vast Wasteland: A Pointless Task," in *The Eight Blindspots of Television News* (Washington: Media Institute, 1992), p. 23.
[2]Ibid.

widest possible audience, it would never be more than "wires and lights in a box."

Given the structure of the early television industry, however, that approach was nothing if not profitable. Through much of the 1950s, CBS and NBC had the national audience to themselves. The percentage of TV homes was still growing when ABC pieced together a third network with many affiliates in the less desirable UHF band. ABC was the upstart—it made its name in sports, not news, and its entertainment programming was a bit less conventional and aimed at a younger audience. The strategy put ABC on the video map, and it was a formula that the Fox Network would follow in large measure some three decades later. During the 1960s, the three networks commanded upward of 95 percent of the national audience. There was no competition from other media; TV, in fact, *was* the competition. The tube was one of the factors that helped turn neighborhood theaters into boarded-up shells and parking lots, and some newspapers refused to print TV listings for fear of aiding the competition. (They need not have worried.) Still, people were not required to sit in front of the set for hours on end. Yet, they did for one simple reason: Television was entertaining. There is nothing wrong with being entertained by TV, of course. It is fun for the viewer and it attracts the large number of people that advertisers covet. But as Neil Postman points out, television's preoccupation with entertainment has a dark side:

> The problem is not that television presents us with entertaining subject matter but that all subject matter is presented as entertaining, which is another issue altogether. . . . Entertainment is the supra-ideology of all discourse on television. No matter what is depicted or from what point of view, the overarching presumption is that it is there for our amusement and pleasure.[3]

Upping the Ante: Sensationalism

Television-as-entertainment was the norm through the 1960s and early 1970s. The economics of the industry were good. The number

[3]Neil Postman, *Amusing Ourselves to Death: Public Discourse in the Age of Show Business* (New York: Viking Penguin, 1985), p. 87.

of TV viewers continued to rise as the population grew, advertising revenues climbed, and the three networks had the audience and the ad dollars to themselves. But the economics began to shift in the 1970s, beginning as a gentle slide and accelerating into a free fall that crashed into the 1990s. The dynamics of the marketplace were changing. Independent stations (mostly in the UHF band) grew rapidly in number from 90 in 1970 to 483 by 1993, fueled largely by old movies and syndicated reruns of network shows. At the same time, cable television was evolving from an antenna technology into a programming service and becoming the fastest-growing segment of the television industry. Suddenly viewers could flip to the far reaches of the dial and find more than static, even if it was reruns of *Gomer Pyle* and *Mister Ed*. The invincible audience share of the networks began to slip. The networks were dealt another blow in the 1980s by videocassette players and video game systems that kept TV sets occupied for hours at a time, often during prime time. Broadcasters still needed to attract mass numbers, but their audiences were becoming increasingly fragmented by the explosion of viewing choices.

Broadcasters, desperate to keep their viewers, tried to make their programming more compelling, attention getting, and even sensational. On the entertainment side, network standards for taste and propriety were relaxed markedly in an attempt to lure viewers back from cable and its less restrictive standards. Hardly a taboo went unexplored in the networks' made-for-TV movies—rape, incest, child abuse, spouse abuse, every addiction, and a great many diseases found their way into America's living rooms. The economics of the industry had changed, and broadcasters responded by making their programs more sensational in an attempt to halt the erosion of audience size and revenues.

Pressures on TV News

The evolution of broadcasting economics and the accompanying change in programming zeitgeist did not bypass the TV newsroom. The first network newscasts were pretty dull affairs, populated by talking heads seated at desks (not fancy "news centers") who might get up and point at a map or talk to a foreign correspondent via a static-filled telephone hookup. Moving pictures were on film and often a day old. Early TV news could be thought of as "radio news meets newsreel." It was dull but informative, it was a public service of the networks, and it was over in 15 minutes. In time, however, entertainment values crept in and ultimately took over; "TV news" became a genre unto itself that learned to take advantage of the power and appeal of the moving image. Information lost out to entertainment. In the early 1970s, NBC News president Reuven Frank was quoted as saying:

> Every news story should, without any sacrifice of probity or responsibility, display the attributes of fiction, of drama. It should have structure and conflict, problem and denouement, rising action and falling action, a beginning, a middle and an end.[4]

Postman puts the blame on TV's visual imagery:

> A news show, to put it plainly, is a format for entertainment, not for education, reflection or catharsis. . . . There is no conspiracy here, no lack of intelligence, only a straightforward recognition that "good television" has . . . everything to do with what the pictorial images look like.[5]

Many words have been written about the shortcomings of TV news: It is too superficial, too dramatic, and too crisis oriented. Even Alfred Sikes, as chairman of the FCC, weighed in with an unusual indictment of program content that he called the "eight blindspots" of TV news.[6] For our discussion here, we would say only that broadcast news requires a mass audience owing to the economics of over-the-air television. The prevailing standards, then, are not those of journalistic ethics but of "good television" that make news visually compelling and dramatically appealing to the masses.

Newsmagazine and Tabloid Journalism

Like entertainment programming generally, television news in recent years has made the switch from being merely entertaining to

---

[4]Quoted in Jeffrey Olen, *Ethics in Journalism* (Englewood Cliffs, N.J.: Prentice-Hall, 1988), p. 105.

[5]Postman, pp. 87–88.

[6]Alfred C. Sikes, "Debt, Deficits, and the Eight Blindspots of Television News," keynote address before the Edward R. Murrow Symposium, Washington State University, April 24, 1992. Reprinted with additional commentary as *The Eight Blindspots of Television News*.

being frequently sensational. Until the video explosion of cable, satellite, and other distribution services took hold in the mid-1980s, news departments were something of a loss leader for the three networks. News budgets were lavish, bureaus were well stocked with both people and equipment, and a certain freewheeling atmosphere prevailed. As competition from cable and other sources cut into viewership and ad revenues, however, budgets were slashed, staffs were cut, and newsrooms entered an unfamiliar age of austerity. News operations were no longer subsidized; they became network profit centers and were expected to pull their own weight.

And thus began in earnest the age of sensationalism, spearheaded by a spate of "newsmagazine" shows. For years, NBC and ABC had been envious of CBS's financial success with *60 Minutes*. Not only was the show consistently at or near the top of the ratings but it was a huge moneymaker for the network. ABC has had some success with *20/20* (which now nets a reported $40 million per year), while NBC tried one unsuccessful magazine format after another. Today, there are no fewer than 10 magazine shows on the three networks, with another four distributed by syndicators.

Shows like *48 Hours, Turning Point, Dateline NBC,* and *Eye to Eye* have much in common, starting with celebrity talent such as Barbara Walters, Diane Sawyer, Jane Pauley, and Connie Chung. The shows are relatively cheap to produce, they can be immensely profitable, and they all brew what *Newsweek* calls the "TV news-magazine elixir: crime and sex, mixed in with sex and crime."[7] ABC, for instance, enticed viewers to the debut of *Turning Point* (with Diane Sawyer) by running a segment on Charles Manson and his women followers. Topics are readily interchangeable: perennial favorites include unscrupulous doctors, victims of abuse, consumer scams, and anything to do with Michael Jackson, serial killer Jeffrey Dahmer (now deceased), and 1993's tabloid triplets Amy Fisher, Lorena Bobbit, and Tonya Harding. The assault on viewers' sensibilities is a far cry from the days when *60 Minutes* was the only magazine show in sight:

> New shows are pouring into the airwaves and, reminiscent of an old-fashioned tabloid war, engaging in what looks like a frenzied search for attention, impact and spectacular

[7]Larry Reibstein, "The Battle of the TV News Magazine Shows," *Newsweek*, April 11, 1994, p. 62. See also Howard Kurtz, "Sex! Mayhem! 'Now'!" *Washington Post*, March 14, 1994, p. D1.

ratings—and not necessarily for the better . . . . The news magazines concede that including the occasional sleazier story is the price to be paid for higher ratings.[8]

The shows that first elevated sleaze to an art form, however, are the syndicated "tabloid" shows—*A Current Affair, Inside Edition, Hard Copy,* and *American Journal.* Like the supermarket tabloids, these shows snag the most sensational stories by paying willing subjects to tell all. This "checkbook journalism" is still frowned upon by the networks, but will competitive pressures and the need to attract viewers with ever-sleazier stories force the networks over the line?

In looking at the state of broadcast news, one can see how network news programming has reflected the changing economics of the Big Three, going from a subsidized public service to another form of entertainment to—in some quarters—the merely sensational. And sensationalism poses a special threat to ethical conduct, especially in the areas of fairness and invasion of privacy. It is unfortunate that journalistic ethics have been squeezed more and more from the picture as news organizations have been forced to bear a greater responsibility for the bottom line.

The answer, however, is *not* more government regulation of the networks. As in most instances involving speech (and government attempts to control it), the preferable solution is *more* speech rather than less. In this case, more speech means the development of additional channels of programming in media that, unlike broadcasting, are more conducive to the practice of journalistic ethics.

Cable Programming: Ethical Opportunities

Because the economics of cable television are fundamentally different from those of broadcasting (i.e., multichannel capacity and a dual revenue stream—advertising and subscriber fees), cable operators are able to offer programming that is substantially different from network fare. The distinguishing characteristic is that cable programming can appeal to relatively small audiences and still be commercially viable (owing to the dual revenue stream). This squares perfectly with the fact that cable is a multichannel technology; a cable system has the channel capacity to accommodate a large number of

[8]Reibstein, pp. 62, 64.

program services, each of which need attract only a small audience (by network standards) to be successful. Imagine a broadcast network that could offer 40 programs at once, instead of only 1. It could broadcast a wide range of programming that appealed to 40 different interests among its audience, instead of trying to find 1 program that everyone liked.

This is exactly what a cable system is able to do. This "narrowcasting," or ability to target narrow segments of the audience with specialized programming, is the great strength of cable television. The basic service of a typical cable system might include channels such as ESPN (the all-sports network); CNBC (consumer and business news); MTV (contemporary music); The Learning Channel, Lifetime, Arts & Entertainment, and USA (movies, comedy, and drama); The Discovery Channel, The Disney Channel, and Nickelodeon (family and children's shows); and CNN and C-SPAN (news and public affairs). In addition, there may be channels targeting interests such as country music, science fiction, court proceedings, foreign-language programming, weather, and regional sports. One would never see this breadth of programming on the Big Three networks, yet scores of shows are happily ensconced on cable where they can prosper by appealing to small, specialized audiences.

News and Public Affairs

Nowhere is cable's narrowcasting advantage more pronounced than in the realm of news and public affairs. And the stars in this galaxy are the Cable News Network, C-SPAN, and CNBC. When CNN debuted in 1980, the idea of filling a channel with 24 hours of news every day seemed daunting—yet Ted Turner proved that such a feat could be achieved, *and* that there was a market of news junkies to support it. From the beginning, CNN offered the prospect of dramatic improvement in both the quantity and quality of televised news. It had the capability of going "live" at any time of day or night with breaking stories, be they modest or momentous; moreover, it promised to deliver vastly more news than its broadcast competitors ever could. CNN went about this task by establishing an impressive string of bureaus both in this country and abroad, just at the time the networks were cutting costs and scaling back their news operations. Just as radio news came of age in World War II and network television news had its Vietnam, CNN emerged as the definitive source of news in Operation Desert Storm in 1992. It was the first war in history in which military commanders on both sides were able to watch real-time televised accounts of the fight and use those accounts as a source of battlefield intelligence.

C-SPAN, in contrast, operates on a different scale but fills no less of a public need. This operation, pioneered by Brian Lamb, made its mark by televising the proceedings of the U.S. Congress out of a belief that the workings of government should be accessible to the public. Public affairs discussion shows rotated hosts because Lamb eschewed broadcasting's cult of personality and did not want a "name" host overshadowing a program's substance. Even today, C-SPAN's production values are primitive by network standards. It may use a single camera to cover a speech, luncheon address, or conference panel in the Washington area. This approach may make for tedious viewing (the ultimate in "talking heads") but C-SPAN has attracted a fanatically loyal viewership scattered throughout the country.

It should come as no surprise that serious news operations like CNN and C-SPAN have attracted significant audiences of serious news consumers. For example, the three broadcast networks have abandoned gavel-to-gavel coverage of the Democratic and Republican national conventions. Preempting profitable entertainment programming can no longer be justified except under the most extreme circumstances. What is a student of the democratic process to do? Turn to C-SPAN or CNN, of course, the only places where extended coverage of the conventions can now be found. The ability to offer long-form coverage is one of the great strengths of these networks. The Gulf War, the standoff with cult leader David Koresh in Waco, Texas, and the confirmation hearings of Clarence Thomas for the Supreme Court are examples of news events that were covered extensively—and best—by these cable outlets.

Narrowcasting and Journalistic Ethics

Because cable enjoys a dual revenue stream and does not require a mass audience, cable programmers do not face the same commercial pressures to select and package news according to entertainment standards. And because cable time is plentiful, programmers have the luxury of presenting a 20-minute speech in its entirety rather than a 20-second sound bite of the speech. The average viewer may find cable news less entertaining than network news, but paradoxically, die-hard news junkies find the cable channels *more* entertaining, precisely because they are getting more of what they want—news and information stripped of the theatricals and presented for substantive rather than entertainment value. That is the essence of narrowcasting.

Not only can cable news be less "entertaining," but it need not rely on the sensationalism that has plagued local newscasts for years and crept into network newsmagazines (and to a lesser extent network nightly newscasts) more recently. An early study of CNN news content, for example, found that the cable network's business and economic coverage was less sensational than that of the broadcast networks.[9] And anyone who has watched C-SPAN knows that its idea of "sensational" might be the roll call vote on the North American Free Trade Agreement or a panel debate on health care reform.

This ability to deliver news and public affairs programming without an emphasis on sensationalism has critical implications for ethical conduct. Simply put, the process of ethical decisionmaking breaks down and even becomes moot in a news environment that places a premium on sensationalism, both in selection of topics and techniques of presentation. When Charles Manson on ABC's *Turning Point* draws three times as many viewers as Peter Jennings's special on Bosnia, what ethical questions are left? Who can argue with the bottom line? Sensationalism is the antithesis of ethical conduct and is the particular nemesis of the ethical principles of fairness and respect for privacy. Borrowing a technique from the tabloid shows, CBS recently used a hidden camera to tape secret footage inside a South Dakota meatpacking plant.[10] The result was a sensational exposé, but was it ethical? (The legality of hidden cameras is another matter altogether.)

Through those and other examples, it becomes clear that cable news organizations offer an environment where journalism can be practiced in a way that is more accommodating of ethical considerations and

---

[9]See *CNN vs. the Networks: Is More News Better News?* (Washington: Media Institute, 1983). Recently, however, CNN came under attack for sensationalizing coverage of child abuse accusations—later proved false—against Cardinal Joseph Bernardin of Chicago. See Mary Ann Walsh, "A 'Scoop' Implausible on Its Face," *Washington Post*, April 15, 1994, p. A25.

[10]Lyle Denniston, "Going Too Far With the Hidden Camera?" *American Journalism Review*, April 1994, p. 54.

less influenced by the commercial pressures besetting broadcasters. But cable television is a technology that the federal government succeeded in stifling for years and still holds in check. By retarding the development of this technology, however, the government has also retarded an opportunity for the development of journalistic ethics.

Stifling Cable Development

The federal government did not set about regulating cable television for the purpose of impeding journalistic ethics. Indeed, the idea that cable might have something to do with newsroom ethics probably never crossed the minds of regulators (or cable operators for that matter), any more than the notion that cable might be connected somehow to the First Amendment. The FCC expanded its regulatory control to cable for two reasons: to please broadcasters, the FCC's historical constituency who had begun to fear competition from the upstart technology; and to please members of Congress, who feared the new medium would not offer them the same access and other privileges they had conferred upon themselves at the expense of broadcasters.

Hundreds of the earliest cable systems were built by telephone companies. By the late 1960s, however, AT&T, GTE, United, Continental, and other phone companies had been effectively driven out of the cable business by FCC requirements that thwarted system expansion. Earlier, the FCC had addressed the concerns of broadcasters who opposed cable operators' growing practice of importing distant signals via microwave transmission facilities. Beginning in 1962, cable operators had to prove that their delivery of distant signals would not harm local broadcasters. By 1966, all cable operators were subject to "must carry" regulations that required cable systems to carry local broadcast signals.[11] But all of that was a mere prelude to the roller coaster of regulation that would restrain cable's growth for the next decade.

No single document did more to freeze cable development than the FCC's *Second Report and Order* issued in 1966.[12] The order said

---

[11]See *Carter Mountain Transmission Corp.*, 32 F.C.C. 459 (1962), *aff'd*, 321 F.2d 359 (D.C. Cir. 1963), *cert. denied*, 375 U.S. 951. See also, for example, *Quincy Cable TV, Inc. v. FCC*, 768 F.2d 1434, 1440 n.11 (D.C. Cir. 1985).

[12]FCC, *Second Report and Order in Dockets 14895, 15233, and 15971*, 2 F.C.C. 2d 725 (1966).

that no cable operator in the top 100 markets could import distant signals without first going through an FCC evidentiary hearing to determine the impact on over-the-air broadcasting. Keeping cable out of the top 100 markets served the interests of established broadcasters who held VHF channel slots in major cities. In 1968, the Supreme Court upheld the FCC's ban on distant signals in *U.S. v. Southwestern Cable Co.*,[13] a case that served the FCC's larger purpose of legitimizing its regulation of cable.

At the commission, meanwhile, enterprising staff members were finding a way around the hearings morass by granting waivers to cable companies in the top 100 markets, allowing them to import distant signals. In 1968, however, the FCC launched a new rulemaking proposal and notice of inquiry that effectively put a stop to further waivers. A new requirement was proposed—that the programming of an out-of-market station could not be carried unless written permission of the station, that is, retransmission consent, was first obtained.[14] But this requirement proved unworkable, thereby keeping cable development stalled.

At the same time that the FCC was holding back the development of cable, it was imposing additional regulations on cable operators as if they were broadcasters. The Fairness Doctrine and the equal opportunities rule were extended to cable in 1969, as well as requirements for program origination.[15] A year later, the FCC added prohibitions against cable operators' owning telephone companies, translator stations, broadcast TV stations, and interests in TV networks within their service areas.

In 1970, the FCC allowed cable operators in major markets to import up to four out-of-market stations, with one hitch—the commercials had to be deleted, and the cable operator had to substitute commercials from local UHF stations.[16] Although the program was subsequently abandoned, "the result was to hold off for another two years cable's ability to increase the number of broadcast television stations that could be carried."[17] In 1972, the commission issued a

[13]*U.S. v. Southwestern Cable Co.*, 392 U.S. 157 (1968).

[14]See FCC, *Notice of Proposed Rule Making and Notice of Inquiry in Docket 18397*, 15 F.C.C. 2d 417 (1968).

[15]See FCC, *Cable Television*, 20 F.C.C. 2d 201, 218–219, 222–223 (1969).

[16]See FCC, *Notice of Proposed Rule Making in Docket 18894*, 25 F.C.C. 2d 38 (1970).

[17]*Turner Broadcasting System, Inc. v. FCC*, amicus curiae brief of the Media Institute before the U.S. Supreme Court (1993), at 21.

Cable Television Report and Order that permitted cable operators to carry up to three distant signals depending on the size of the television market.[18] The order also imposed a host of other cable regulations that were subsequently modified in 1975.[19]

The FCC's long-standing campaign to favor broadcasters at the expense of cable operators suffered a major setback in 1985 in *Quincy Cable TV, Inc. v. FCC.*[20] The D.C. Circuit Court ruled that the FCC's must-carry rules were invalid. These rules, first articulated in 1962 and applied to all cable systems in 1966, required cable operators to carry the signals of local broadcast stations. Apparently undaunted, the commission set about the task of aiding broadcasters in a way that would withstand judicial scrutiny. Two years later (1987), the FCC unveiled revised rules but the D.C. Circuit Court intervened again. In *Century Communications Corp. v. FCC*, the court ruled that the revised plan failed the constitutional analysis applied in *Quincy.*[21] This decision effectively stalled FCC efforts to pursue the must-carry fight.

Congress joined the cable fray in 1984 by enacting legislation that was hailed at the time as "deregulating" the cable industry.[22] In reality, it merely formalized the fact that regulatory authority resided in local franchising authorities and essentially told local authorities how much they could extract from cable operators. The act condoned "exclusive franchising," and allowed municipalities to commandeer cable channels "for public, educational, or governmental use." In exchange for a 5 percent cap on franchise fees, cable operators were allowed a free hand in setting subscriber rates except in cases where "effective competition" did not exist. In essence, the cable industry was willing to settle for legislation that granted rate-setting freedom in exchange for continued regulation related to the franchising process, channel usage, and franchising fees. The *Cable Communications*

---

[18]FCC, *Cable Television Report and Order*, 36 F.C.C. 2d 143 (1972).

[19]See FCC, *Major Market Cable Television Systems*, 54 F.C.C. 2d 207 (1975). See also *Cable TV Capacity and Access Requirements*, 59 F.C.C. 2d 294 (1976).

[20]*Quincy Cable TV, Inc. v. FCC*, 768 F.2d 1434 (D.C. Cir. 1985), *cert. denied*, 476 U.S. 1169 (1986).

[21]*Century Communications Corp. v. FCC*, 835 F.2d 292 (D.C. Cir. 1987), *cert. denied*, 486 U.S. 1032 (1988).

[22]*Cable Communications Policy Act of 1984*, Pub. L. No. 98–549, 98 Stat. 2779, codified at 47 U.S.C. Secs. 521 et seq.

Policy Act of 1984 marked the first major effort of Congress to backstop the FCC in keeping the now-burgeoning cable industry in check.

Current Impediments to Cable Development

The government's appetite for stifling cable growth was not sated by the 1984 Cable Act any more than it was dulled by court rulings against must carry. Members of Congress, led by Rep. Edward J. Markey (D-Mass.), headed a chorus eager to "reregulate" the cable industry—that is, reimpose price controls, keep all other restrictions in place, and find a way to work in must carry to make the broadcasters happy.

This effort reached fruition in the *Cable Television Consumer Protection and Competition Act of 1992.*[23] This act, the subject of intense and prolonged lobbying on all sides, effectively reimposed rate regulation. The act also offered a unique approach to the old question of retransmission consent versus must carry: it gave broadcasters the right to demand either option. Following the initial round of broadcaster elections, it emerged that network affiliates and popular independents were in a position to negotiate retransmission consent deals (i.e., demand payments from cable operators), while lesser independents (generally UHF stations) opted for the security of must carry.[24]

The 1992 Cable Act had the additional effect of breathing new life into the must-carry debate. The must-carry provisions of the act were challenged in U.S. district court (D.C.), which held that must carry was economic regulation (rather than regulation of speech) and was constitutional under the *O'Brien* test. In June 1994, the Supreme Court concurred that the regulations were content neutral and that *O'Brien* was the correct standard, and remanded the case to the district court for further development of the record.[25]

The FCC could hardly think of a better way to stifle the cable industry's long-term growth than to choke back its revenue stream.

---

[23]*Cable Television Consumer Protection and Competition Act of 1992,* Pub. L. No. 102–385, 106 Stat. 1,460, amending 47 U.S.C. Secs. 521 et seq.

[24]For a thorough discussion of the 1992 Cable Act's provisions and implications, see Sol Schildhause and Howard Liberman, eds. *Arter & Hadden's Cable TV Act of 1992 Sourcebook* (Washington: Arter & Hadden, 1993).

[25]*Turner Broadcasting System, Inc. v. FCC,* 1994 U.S. Lexis 4831 (June 27, 1994) *vacating* 819 F. Supp. 32 (D.D.C. 1993). See *United States v. O'Brien,* 391 U.S. 367 (1968).

Yet, this is precisely what the commission did in early 1993 and again in 1994. The rate rollbacks were a one-two punch that left the industry reeling and threatened to knock out some smaller systems for the count.

The genesis of the rollbacks was the 1992 Cable Act, which directed the FCC to set standards for the cable rates of systems that did not face effective competition. On April 1, 1993, the FCC stunned the industry by announcing a 6 month rate freeze and a 10 percent rollback of rates that exceeded FCC benchmarks. Rates in effect on September 30, 1992, were to be cut 10 percent or rolled back to a benchmark rate (whichever was less), yet no benchmark had been devised at the time of the announcement.[26] The problem was compounded by the fact that the benchmarks issued months later by the FCC were nearly unintelligible, leading to a compliance fiasco. In the summer of 1993, the commission hired 75 extra lawyers just to sort through the deluge of cable rate filings. Robert Pepper, director of the FCC's Office of Policy and Planning, predicted the regulatory effort would cost the agency an extra $12 million in 1993 and $16 million in 1994.[27] The investment community reacted quickly and negatively to the FCC's announcement. The stock value of 11 multiple-system operators tracked by Paul Kagan Associates dropped $5.8 billion in just two days—even though the FCC was predicting the rollback would cost cable systems $1 billion to $1.5 billion in lost cash flow annually.[28]

The FCC's meddling in the economics of the cable marketplace had a huge and untoward impact: it caused a serious reduction in operating revenues; depressed stock prices, thereby leading to a devaluation of the entire industry; threatened the survival of systems that were highly leveraged or operating on thin margins;[29] caused credit to dry up; imposed intolerable compliance burdens on cable

[26]"FCC Calls for Rate Freeze and Rollbacks," *Paul Kagan Cable TV Regulation News Bulletin*, April 5, 1993, p. 1.

[27]Ibid., p. 5.

[28]"FCC Lowers Boom on Cable Operators; MSO Stocks Nosedive," *Paul Kagan Cable TV Investor News Analysis*, April 2, 1993, p. 1.

[29]One of the first casualties was Green River Cable TV in Russell Springs, Kentucky. The 1,400-subscriber system filed for Chapter 11 bankruptcy protection in April 1994 because the continuing rate freeze made it impossible to repay $1.25 million in bank loans. See Kate Maddox, "Endangered Cable Firms Eye Options," *Electronic Media*, May 2, 1994, p. 3.

operators who found themselves caught in a labyrinth of paperwork, and slowed the rollout of new program services. Acting at the bidding of Congress, the FCC decimated the cable industry so that politicians like Representative Markey could boast that they were helping consumers save a few dollars. But were consumers being helped or hurt? The National Cable Television Association (NCTA) estimated that the initial $2 billion in lost revenues would have financed system upgrades for 7.8 million subscribers or the creation of 40 new basic cable program services.[30]

Having hammered the industry for a full year, the FCC regrouped—and then unleashed another barrage. In late March 1994, the agency announced that it was scrapping the 10 percent rollback and implementing a new plan that would cut cable rates by 17 percent. The new formula would be based on 10 variables and require 3 logarithmic equations to arrive at the benchmark, from which 17 percent would be deducted.[31] The old formula, which was incomprehensible enough, was based on only three variables. Rules for the new 17 percent cut filled over 500 pages.

The FCC admitted that the decision to adopt the 17 percent figure was political rather than economic. "The idea that 17 percent is the right competitive differential is basically a policy judgment. . . . There's not a formula for 17 percent," said FCC economist Jonathan Levy.[32] The commission had considered competitive differentials as high as 37 percent and was under intense pressure from Congress to cut rates substantially more than the original 10 percent.

By cutting cable rates to appease the short-term interests of consumers (i.e., voters), the FCC and Congress have jeopardized the long-term growth of the cable industry. Cable industry leaders were quick to voice this concern. Reducing the industry's revenues "cannot help but reduce our options when it comes to introducing new programming, new services and new technologies," said NCTA president Decker Anstrom.[33] "This will stymie the production of

[30]"Myhren Criticizes FCC Cable Rate Plans," *Broadcasting & Cable*, February 21, 1994, p. 6.

[31]John M. Higgins and Ted Hearn, "FCC's New Math as Easy as Trig," *Multichannel News*, April 4, 1994, p. 54.

[32]Jenny Hontz, "Analysts Criticize How FCC Figured Rollback Formula," *Electronic Media*, April 11, 1994, p. 23.

[33]Higgins and Hearn, p. 54.

new programming, which is the lifeblood of this industry," said J.C. Sparkman, TCI executive vice president and executive officer.[34] The president of the Arts & Entertainment Network said the rollback would threaten the debut of the proposed History Channel and warned that "we may have already seen the last new cable programming network of value."[35]

The implications here for journalistic ethics are not promising. A reduction in subscriber revenues could easily mean that the cable industry is forced to place a greater emphasis on advertising revenues with the concomitant need to attract ever-larger audiences. System operators will have less revenue with which to develop innovative local news and public affairs shows. And there will be less incentive to develop national news and public affairs programming unless it can attract audiences sufficiently large to help offset losses in subscriber fees. Cable television, perhaps the most promising electronic environment for journalistic ethics, could itself turn out to be nothing more than "wires and lights in a box." It would be ironic and unfortunate if this occurred just as cable was preparing to become a major thoroughfare on the information superhighway.

[34]Kate Maddox, "Cable Struggles With FCC Rules," *Electronic Media*, April 11, 1994, p. 23.

[35]Nickolas Davatzes, "Quality Cable at Risk," *Washington Post*, April 27, 1994, p. A23.

5. Journalistic Ethics and the Information Superhighway

Much has been written about the future of telecommunications and the various forms that media of the 21st century may take. We will not attempt an exhaustive discussion of this book-length topic here except to note some likely trends and to consider the implications for journalistic ethics, especially in light of continued government meddling in the communication industry's structure and economics.

The Information Superhighway

We are entering a media age that will be characterized by three factors: convergence, interactivity, and digitization. Convergence refers to the blurring of lines among technologies as we currently know them. The day will come when a consumer accesses entertainment programming (at fixed times and on demand), telephone service, news programming, and database information services through a single company. This provider may originally have been a phone company or a cable system but its state-of-the-art infrastructure is now each individual's personal pathway to the information superhighway. And the point of convergence is the individual's computer and audio-video monitor where entertainment and information data are received, manipulated, stored, and transmitted.

Interactivity refers to two-way communication. An individual will no longer be merely a passive recipient of information but will be able to access vast stores of data about virtually any topic. Breaking news will be instantly accessible in a choice of audio, video, and graphic formats, with huge amounts of background data available at the user's command. One will no longer have to wait until an appointed hour to view a newscast; a stream of information bits will be constantly available. This interactivity will be made possible by advanced over-the-air and wire technologies (such as fiber optics) with the capacity to handle large amounts of data moving in both directions, and by the conversion of information processing to digital systems. Movies, scholarly texts, phone conversations, baseball games, financial data, and breaking news will all move throughout the information infrastructure with equal and indistinguishable ease as digitized dots and dashes. The infrastructure, in fact, may not resemble a highway much at all:

> The emerging information infrastructure will more closely resemble the loosely organized, interactive Internet than the switched telephone network or one-way broadcasting system. Instead of a linear highway, the new information infrastructure will be more like a vast parking lot on which anyone will be free to travel in any direction, wherever and whenever they please.[1]

By early 1994, however, the Clinton administration announced its desire to be the architect of the information superhighway. President Clinton unveiled plans for a "National Information Infrastructure" and placed Vice President Gore in charge of the project. Gore said the administration would introduce legislation early in 1994, but none had been forthcoming by August. Legislation had already been introduced by Representatives Edward J. Markey (D-Mass.) and Jack Fields (R-Tex.) that would, among other things, allow telephone companies to offer in-region cable service and require local phone companies to offer access and interconnection to their networks. This proposal found itself competing with an earlier bill by Representatives Jack Brooks (D-Tex.) and John D. Dingell (D-Mich.) that would eventually allow regional phone companies to offer long-distance service, provide cable service, and manufacture equipment.[2] Both bills passed the House. A bill introduced by Sen. Ernest F. Hollings

---

[1]David Bartlett, "The Soul of a News Machine: Electronic Journalism in the 21st Century," paper presented at the Federal Communications Bar Association seminar, February 4, 1994, p. 4. See also, for example, Charles M. Firestone, ed., *Television for the 21st Century: The Next Wave* (Washington: Aspen Institute, 1993).

[2]See, for example, Kim McAvoy, "Full Speed Ahead on Superhighway," *Broadcasting & Cable*, January 10, 1994, p. 10; Christopher Stern, "Additions May Delay Telecommunications Bill," *Broadcasting & Cable*, March 21, 1994, p. 60; and Kim McAvoy, "Hill May Not Get to Info Highway This Year," *Broadcasting & Cable*, April 18, 1994, p. 13.

(D-S.C.) addressed similar issues in the Senate, but no legislation reached the President's desk in 1994.[3]

Such initiatives can be viewed as attempts by the federal government to foster a competitive and technologically advanced communications industry. Or they can be viewed for what they really are: attempts by the Clinton administration and Congress to take credit for what the industry is already doing; or efforts to relax regulations that should never have been imposed in the first place—while imposing still other restrictions.

The government's exhortations in favor of an information superhighway are especially suspect given its actual performance, particularly regarding the 17 percent rollback of cable rates. Among the first casualties of that decision were pending deals that would have created the first "superhighway" companies of the future. One day after the additional 7 percent cut was announced, TCI and Bell Atlantic scrapped plans for a $30 billion deal in which Bell Atlantic would have taken over the cable giant in the biggest deal in American business history.[4] The rate reduction's impact on cash flow was cited as a primary reason for the deal's failure. The rollback was also blamed for the collapse of a proposed $4.9 billion joint venture between Southwestern Bell and Cox Cable.[5] And a $12.6 billion merger between AT&T and McCaw Cellular found itself bogged down in a different batch of Washington red tape.[6] AT&T's actions are still subject to approval by the U.S. district court that oversaw the breakup of the Bell system in 1983—and those approvals can be excruciatingly slow if they come at all. The Justice Department has a separate review and waiver process for antitrust concerns, while the FCC itself can create still other logjams. In early 1994, for example, the agency was sitting on 17 requests for interactive video service tests, some of which had been languishing for over a year.[7]

---

[3]Jenny Hontz, "Infohighway Bill Hits Roadblock," *Electronic Media*, August 1, 1994, p. 3.

[4]Christopher Stern, "Abrupt End to the Beginning," *Broadcasting & Cable*, February 28, 1994, p. 6.

[5]John M. Higgins and Kent Gibbons, "Cox–SW Bell Deal's Collapse Yields Fear," *Multichannel News*, April 11, 1994, p. 1.

[6]John J. Keller, Leslie Cauley, and Mary Lu Carnevale, "Washington Slows Speed on Information Superhighway," *Wall Street Journal*, April 8, 1994, p. B1.

[7]Ibid., p. B6.

The FCC chairman promised an all-out drive to process the pending requests.

Impact on Ethics

The information superhighway, with its convergence of technologies and interactive capabilities, will cause profound changes in the ways news is gathered and disseminated. News will become a creature of the technologies delivering it—"superhighway news" will become a different and distinct news genre just as broadcast technology created a genre called "television news" that differed from newspapers in substance as well as form. This new breed of news will be characterized by more information from more sources:

> The 21st century news machine will be an interactive, multimedia system possessing the power of television, the portability of newspapers, and the flexible structure of the telephone network. . . . More and more separate news organizations will appear, each a good deal smaller and more specialized than those we see today. From these smaller and more efficient news operations will emerge a far greater volume and variety of news aimed at much smaller audiences. . . . The very notion of "mass" media will fade into history. . . . The next generation of news producers will spend more of their time cataloging and classifying information than actually gathering it.[8]

The role of most journalists will change from gatekeeper and filter of information (news-limiting functions) to facilitator and packager of information (news-expediting functions). This change will pose new ethical questions: If a journalist loads a database with all available information on a subject, for example, is he or she relieved of the ethical duty to strive for fairness? Fairness, after all, involves judgments about which facts should be included and omitted when the space or time for presentation is limited. Fairness is a concern based on scarcity, occasioned by the limited resources of time and space available for news presentation; will it still apply in an information environment that offers unlimited capacity?

In another respect, and closer in time to the present, a decentralized information infrastructure featuring many small news organizations

---

[8]Bartlett, pp. 5, 6–7.

should offer a nurturing environment for journalistic ethics. Small audiences, niche reporting strategies, and multiple revenue streams (subscriber fees, advertising, and perhaps pay-as-you-go fees for ancillary information services) should create an environment in which journalists have a greater chance of producing programming that is free of sensationalism and the ethical abuses it invites. Such a setting, not unlike today's cable narrowcasting, should help avoid some of the conditions that currently jeopardize ethical conduct in network news organizations: severe restraints on time and the need to attract a mass audience at any cost.

The presence of many small news organizations should also give consumers a greater role in shaping journalistic ethics. Those who want more objectivity and less sensationalism, for example, will be able to switch to sources of information and channels of programming that meet the desired level of objectivity. The information superhighway will give consumers far more choices, good and bad. Some individuals will always choose sensationalism. But to the extent that others choose quality journalism, ethical growth will occur as at least some news outlets try to meet that consumer demand for higher standards. Ultimately, the choices of individual consumers in a multisource information marketplace will do more to foster journalistic ethics than any government-imposed system.

This ethical environment, however, will depend on the financial health of the information programmers and distributors of the future. Their financial health, in turn, will depend on their ability to develop competitively without government restraints on industry structure and growth. Thus, perhaps one of the biggest tasks facing those who would foster journalistic ethics will be preventing the federal government from erecting structural barriers that impede the growth of companies attempting to build the information superhighway.

6. Conclusion

Journalistic ethics is a subject that is at once amorphous, ambiguous, and often, it seems, inscrutable. It is an uncomfortable topic for many journalists. A reporter who lacks knowledge of the differences among classical ethical theories is unlikely to appreciate how some of those theories, such as pure rule deontology and rule utilitarianism, can be combined to yield a framework of ethical principles of the sort suggested by Edmund Lambeth and the Society of Professional Journalists. Thus, the reporter may end up acting on the basis of little more than intuition. Or, he may end up following Lambeth's principles of truth telling, justice, freedom, humaneness, and stewardship merely by rote or as a matter of common sense. For the journalist who is ethically motivated, however, this can yield an uncomfortable vagueness about *why* an action is right; difficulty in identifying and analyzing one's assumptions about why an action *seems* right; and an inability to reflect deeply on the underlying ethical principles that could help give cohesion to one's decision-making.

Making the problem worse is that journalists—especially those in the broadcast media—face relentless economic and competitive pressures to present news in a way that attracts the largest number of viewers. Ethical standards thus have to compete with production values that demand the dramatic and entertaining; constraints on time and space; and the consequences of not getting the story at all. (For example, what are the odds that an editor will eventually promote a reporter whose ethical sense of humaneness keeps her from shoving a microphone into the faces of distraught parents and grieving widows?)

Added to this dilemma is the factor we have explored in this publication: the role of government in impeding journalistic ethics. Government stifles ethical development in two ways. First, it creates laws and regulations that in effect take the place of ethical standards, thus substituting a form of "government ethics" for private ethics.

89

The unfortunate effect is that laws and regulations prescribing minimum standards of conduct tend to drive down ethical standards to those minimums. Second, government erects formidable structural barriers to the development of the very technologies that may offer journalists a more hospitable environment for the practice of ethical journalism. Owing to the structure of the cable television industry, for example, cable news organizations can be commercially viable without being "entertaining" or even sensational in the manner of the broadcast networks. (Sensationalism is perhaps the biggest enemy of ethical conduct, threatening the ethical principles of fairness, humaneness, respect of privacy, and even truth telling.) Yet, historically the federal government stifled the development and expansion of cable television for years and continues to impede it today with onerous rate regulations. Meanwhile, telephone companies have been stymied in their attempts to become information companies (which would encompass the provision of news through cable service and interactive technologies) by a labyrinth of laws, agency regulations, consent decrees, and court orders.

One factor has emerged: government actions that hurt the economic well-being of media outlets are potentially hurtful to the practice of quality journalism.

As we survey the field of journalistic ethics and try to reconcile the pursuit of ethics with the technological realities of today and the promises of tomorrow, two conclusions are inescapable. (1) *Dialogue and debate that refine journalists' thinking about ethical principles and how they can best be implemented must continue and in fact expand.* The practice of journalism cries out for standards that are based, at a minimum, on the ethical principles of truth telling, fairness, and humaneness (which includes a respect for the right of privacy). (2) *A hospitable environment must be cultivated in which journalism has the potential to be practiced with a high regard for ethical principles.* Two factors are essential for a healthy ethical climate: media organizations that are financially sound; and the absence of government interference, both directly through laws and regulations and indirectly through structural impediments to industry growth.

Toward the achievement of these two goals—refinements in ethical thinking and a hospitable environment for the practice of ethical journalism—we offer the following recommendations:

- Renew the study of classical ethical theory as the starting point for discussions about journalistic ethics. A journalist cannot be expected to build an ethical framework without a solid foundation.
- Increase the number of opportunities for debate and dialogue between journalists and academicians. Additional conferences, workshops, newsroom roundtables, and other opportunities for journalists to learn from ethicists (and vice versa) are necessary.
- In developing codes of ethics, distinguish clearly between legal requirements and ethical standards; avoid confusing the two. In practice, resist the tendency to let ethical conduct slip to the level of legal compliance.
- Repeal content controls on broadcasters. FCC regulations on equal opportunities, personal attacks, and editorializing are inappropriate government restrictions on program content. Fight efforts to reinstate the Fairness Doctrine, whether as an amendment to the Communications Act or as an FCC rule.
- Continue developing alternatives to the libel law process, such as arbitration and dispute resolution programs. Quick, inexpensive, and efficient means of resolving press disputes will always be a desirable alternative to the judicial process for most people.
- Keep working on libel law reform. Ideal legislation, we believe, would eliminate punitive damages and would provide safeguards for protecting the confidentiality of information generated through other dispute resolution procedures.
- Remove legal and regulatory barriers to a healthy communications industry, starting with existing broadcast networks. Repeal of antiquated regulations, such as the multiple ownership rule, duopoly rule, dual network rule, and cable ownership rule would be a good beginning.
- Repeal the 1992 Cable Act and allow cable systems to set rates in a marketplace environment. At a minimum, cancel the FCC's rate rollbacks based on the 1992 act.
- Remove legal and regulatory restrictions on telephone companies that keep them from competing now and that will slow their efforts to build the information superhighway.

Journalistic ethics do not exist in a vacuum. The development of television news taught us that ethics are influenced by the technological environment in which they are practiced, and that ethics may have to compete (often unsuccessfully) with the unique economic and structural pressures of each medium. This influence has been especially evident in TV network news where such pressures often keep conscientious journalists from practicing what they know to be the highest form of the reporting craft. In recalling the courage of Edward R. Murrow, CBS anchor Dan Rather reflected recently on the state of the journalistic trade that Murrow founded:[1]

> How goes the battle for quality, for truth, and justice, for programs worthy of the *best* within ourselves and the audience? . . . The battle *not* to be merely "wires and lights in a box," the battle to make television *not just* entertaining but also, at least some little of the time, *useful* for higher, better things? How goes the battle?
>
> The answer, we know, is "Not very well." In too many important ways, we have allowed this great instrument, this resource, this weapon for good, to be squandered and cheapened. About this, the best among us hang their heads in embarrassment, even shame. We all should be ashamed of what we have and have not done, measured against what we could do . . . ashamed of many of the things we have allowed our craft, our profession, our life's work to become.[1]

Rather's remarks remind us that ethical standards *do* matter to serious journalists, even if that concern is not immediately visible to the eyes of a public grown accustomed to sensational ethical lapses. In the wake of the *Dateline NBC* scandal involving the rigged pickup truck explosion, NBC News president Michael Gartner was fired "to encourage the others" who had grown complacent about ethical practices.[2] His firing shows that ethical principles *can* be taken seriously, but it also suggests that ethical decisionmaking needs to be a part of every newsroom long before ceremonial beheadings are necessary.

---

[1]Dan Rather, "Call It Courage," presentation at the Radio-Television News Directors Association annual convention, September 29, 1993, pp. 7–8 (emphasis in original).

[2]See, for example, Elizabeth Kolbert, "NBC News Chief Quits to Relieve Network's Pains," *New York Times*, March 3, 1993, p. A1. "To encourage the others" (*pour encourager les autres*), as noted by Voltaire in Chapter 23 of *Candide*. Following an inconclusive engagement with the French at Minorca in 1756, British Admiral John Byng was court-martialed for neglect of duty, sentenced to death, and shot on his own quarterdeck in 1757.

We can no longer ignore the role of government in hindering the development of ethical journalism. Whether by substituting "government ethics" for private ethics, or by creating barriers that stifle industry growth and thereby retard the development of more hospitable ethical environments, government *does* work against the interest of quality journalism.

The government's historical record in this regard is abundantly clear. And this record of controlling content and stifling communications industry growth should sound an alarm to all who care about journalism, who care about the value of an informed electorate in a democracy. This legacy of control belongs to the same government that has already announced its intention to become the architect of this country's information superhighway—our primary conduit of news and information—well into the 21st century.

Index

ABC, 65, 68, 71, 75
Act deontology, 19
Actual malice standard, 49–51
Act utilitarianism, 15
Advertising
  broadcast television, 66–67, 69
  cable television, 66–67
All-Channel Receiver Act, 65
Altruism, 14–15
  See also Utilitarianism
American Arbitration Association, 53
American Journal, 72
American Society of Newspaper
  Editors
  ethics code, 58
  statement of principles, 31n
Annenberg Washington Program in
  Communications Policy Studies, 54
Anstrom, Decker, 81
Arts & Entertainment, 73
Associated Press Managing Editors
  ethics code, 2, 59–60
Audiences
  broadcast television dependence on
    mass, 66–69
  cable television, 67, 69, 72–74
  demands of mass, 64

Barney, Ralph D., 2n, 21, 30–31n, 35n
Bartlett, David, 67n, 84n, 86
Beauchamp, Tom L., 31n
Bedell, Sally, 57
Benjamin, Burton, 57–58
Bentham, Jeremy, 14
Bernadin, Joseph (cardinal), 75n
Bezanson, Randall P., 49, 51, 53, 60
Black, Jay, 2n, 30–31n, 35n
Bobbit, Lorena, 71
Bork, Robert H., 41, 47
Branzburg v. Hayes (1972), 51n
Broadcasting
  FCC rules imposed on, 44–47
  government ethical standards for
    political, 43–44

regulation under FCC Fairness
  Doctrine, 34, 39–40
substitution of FCC ethics for private
  ethics, 44–47
Broadcast television
  development of networks, 65
  economics of, 66–72
  effect on regulation of cable
    television, 76–78
  as entertainment, 68–69
  newsmagazine shows, 71–72
  See also Cable television
Brogan, Patrick, 55n, 56n
Brooks, Jack, 84
Bush administration, 42

Cable Communications Policy Act
  (1984), 78–79
Cable News Network, 73
Cable television
  development and regulation of,
    65–66
  economics of, 66–67, 72–76
  government hindrance of, 3, 64–65
  impact of FCC regulation, 80–82
Cable Television Consumer Protection
  and Competition
  Act (1992), 79–80, 91
Candidates, political, 43–44
Carmody, John, 1n
Carnevale, Mary Lu, 85n
Carter Mountain Transmission Corp.
  (1962), 76n
Cauley, Leslie, 85n
CBS, 1, 52, 57, 65, 68, 71, 75
CBS Benjamin Report, 57–58
  See also Westmoreland v. CBS (1983)
Censorship, 33
  See also Fairness Doctrine
Century Communications Corp. v. FCC
  (1987), 78
Children's Television Act (1990), 34
Chung, Connie, 1, 71
Clinton administration, 42, 47, 84–85
CNBC, 73

95

About the Authors

Richard T. Kaplar is vice president of the Media Institute in Washington, D.C. He has written, edited, or produced over 30 books and monographs on a variety of topics in the communications policy field. Mr. Kaplar is the author of *Advertising Rights, The Neglected Freedom: Toward a New Doctrine of Commercial Speech* (1991), and *The Financial Interest and Syndication Rules: Prime Time for Repeal* (1990). He is the editor of *Bad Prescription for the First Amendment* (1993), and *Beyond the Courtroom: Alternatives for Resolving Press Disputes* (1991). Mr. Kaplar's areas of interest include the First Amendment and freedom of speech; competition and market economics; and government regulation of the communications industry.

Patrick D. Maines has been president and chief executive officer of the Media Institute since 1984. The Institute is a Washington-based nonprofit organization specializing in communications policy and First Amendment issues. A frequent lecturer and editorial contributor to magazines and newspapers, Mr. Maines has created and directed all of the Institute's communications policy and legal activities, with a special interest in First Amendment and new-media issues.

Cato Institute

Founded in 1977, the Cato Institute is a public policy research foundation dedicated to broadening the parameters of policy debate to allow consideration of more options that are consistent with the traditional American principles of limited government, individual liberty, and peace. To that end, the Institute strives to achieve greater involvement of the intelligent, concerned lay public in questions of policy and the proper role of government.

The Institute is named for *Cato's Letters*, libertarian pamphlets that were widely read in the American Colonies in the early 18th century and played a major role in laying the philosophical foundation for the American Revolution.

Despite the achievement of the nation's Founders, today virtually no aspect of life is free from government encroachment. A pervasive intolerance for individual rights is shown by government's arbitrary intrusions into private economic transactions and its disregard for civil liberties.

To counter that trend, the Cato Institute undertakes an extensive publications program that addresses the complete spectrum of policy issues. Books, monographs, and shorter studies are commissioned to examine the federal budget, Social Security, regulation, military spending, international trade, and myriad other issues. Major policy conferences are held throughout the year, from which papers are published thrice yearly in the *Cato Journal*. The Institute also publishes the quarterly magazine *Regulation*.

In order to maintain its independence, the Cato Institute accepts no government funding. Contributions are received from foundations, corporations, and individuals, and other revenue is generated from the sale of publications. The Institute is a nonprofit, tax-exempt, educational foundation under Section 501(c)3 of the Internal Revenue Code.

CATO INSTITUTE
1000 Massachusetts Ave., N.W.
Washington, D.C. 20001

<u>Why</u>
• ensure news tells truth/acts
responsibly (5 pts. — p. 26)